GO GREAT WESTERN

A History of GWR Publicity

ISSUED MONTHLY, UNDER THE AUTHORITY OF THE COMPANY.

JUNE, 1865.]   [PRICE ONE PENNY.

TIME TABLES.

GREAT WESTERN

AND OTHER RAILWAYS IN CONNECTION,

To Bristol, Salisbury, Wells, Weymouth, Gloucester, Cheltenham, Hereford, Cardiff, Newport, Swansea, New Milford, Oxford, Worcester, Malvern, Dudley, Leamington, Warwick, Birmingham, Wolverhampton, Shrewsbury, Chester, Manchester, Birkenhead, & Liverpool.

BRISTOL AND EXETER RAILWAY TO EXETER;
SOUTH DEVON RAILWAY TO PLYMOUTH;
CORNWALL RAILWAY to FALMOUTH;
WEST CORNWALL RAILWAY TO PENZANCE;

And by Steamers viâ MILFORD HAVEN to WATERFORD, viâ HOLYHEAD to KINGSTOWN, viâ WEYMOUTH to GUERNSEY and JERSEY, and viâ BRISTOL to CORK.

CONTENTS.

TIME TABLES—

	PAGE
GENERAL INDEX	2
Notice of alteration of Trains	3
Paddington to Bristol, Exeter, Plymouth, and Penzance	16, 17
Penzance, Plymouth, Exeter, and Bristol, to Paddington	18, 19
Paddington to Oxford, Birmingham, Shrewsbury, Birkenhead, Liverpool, Manchester, &c.	20, 21
Manchester, Liverpool, Birkenhead, Shrewsbury, Birmingham, Oxford, &c., to Paddington	22, 23
Paddington to Worcester, Kidderminster, Dudley, and Wolverhampton	24
Wolverhampton, Dudley, Kidderminster, and Worcester to Paddington	25
Paddington to Worcester, Malvern, Hereford, Abergavenny, and Newport	26
Newport, Abergavenny, Hereford, Malvern, and Worcester to Paddington	27
Paddington to Gloucester, Cheltenham, Cardiff, Swansea, and New Milford (Milford Haven)	28, 29
New Milford (Milford Haven), Swansea, Cardiff, Cheltenham, and Gloucester, to Paddington	30, 31
RETURN TICKETS	5, 8
BYELAWS AND REGULATIONS	7, 8
GOODS AND PARCELS	15
PERIODICAL TICKETS	6
CAB FARES	4
Stratford-upon-Avon Railway	34
Shrewsbury and Hereford, and Hereford, Ross, and Gloucester	32, 33
Wooferton and Tenbury, Tenbury and Bewdley, and Leominster and Kington Branches	34, 35
Llangollen and Corwen Branch	II.
Birkenhead, Chester, and Manchester	II.
Worcester, Bridgnorth, Ironbridge, Wenlock, and Shrewsbury	35
Wellington and Severn Junction, Madeley and Coalbrookdale	35
Bridport Branch	36, 37
London, Chippenham, Westbury, Salisbury, Wells, Yeovil, Dorchester, and Weymouth	36, 37
Devizes Branch	38

	PAGE
Calne Branch	38
London, Brentford, Uxbridge and Windsor	38, 39
Wycombe, Aylesbury, Thame, and Oxford Branch	39
Henley Branch	40
Paddington, Reading, Hungerford, Marlboro', Newbury, Devizes, Weymouth, & Bristol	40
Basingstoke Branch	41
Bristol and South Wales Union Railway	41
Bristol to Exeter	42
Exeter to Plymouth	43
Plymouth to Falmouth	44
Truro to Penzance	44
Tenby and Pembroke Railway	44
Nantwich and Market Drayton Railway	45
Vale of Neath to Merthyr	I.
General Notices	III. V. XVI.

THROUGH COMMUNICATION TABLES—

Pontypool Road, Aberdare, and Swansea	I.
Manchester and G. W. R., viâ Bushbury	IV.
Great Western and Great Eastern	V.
West London Railway	VI. VII.
Chatham and Dover, Brighton, South Western, and G. W. R., viâ West London	VI. VII.
Chester and Holyhead Line—Rhyl, Llandudno, Bangor, &c	VIII.
Dublin, viâ Holyhead	VIII.
IRELAND { Milford Haven	X.
Cork, viâ Bristol	IX.
Londonderry and Belfast, viâ Liverpool	IX.
Channel Islands, viâ Weymouth	XI
Lancaster, Whitehaven, and Carlisle	XII.
London and Abergavenny	XIII.
Metropolitan Railway—Through Trains to and from Great Western Railway	XIV.
Metropolitan and Hammersmith and City Railways	XV.
Through Route over Shrewsbury and Hereford Line	32, 33
Great Western, Midland, and North Eastern	XVI.
COACHES	45, 46, 47
Through Communication between Great-Western and South-Eastern and South-Western Railways viâ Reading	See small Bills at beginning of Book.

LONDON: PRINTED BY HENRY TUCK, 128, ALDERSGATE STREET.

The front page of the June 1865, Great Western Passenger Timetable

GO GREAT WESTERN

A History of GWR Publicity

ROGER BURDETT WILSON

DAVID ST JOHN THOMAS
DAVID & CHARLES

British Library Cataloguing in Publication Data
Wilson, Roger Burdett
    Go Great Western : a history of GWR
    publicity.—2nd ed.
    1. Great Western Railway   2. Advertising—
    Railroads—England—History
    I. Title   II. Judge, C.W. (Colin Walter)
    659.1'938506542   HF6161.R25

    ISBN 0-946537-38-0

For Pat and Margaret Lane,
a tribute to James Grierson

First published in 1970
Second extended edition 1987

Set in 11½ on 13 point Garamond
and printed in Great Britain
by Redwood Burn Ltd, Trowbridge
for David St John Thomas
Distributed by David & Charles Publishers plc
Brunel House Newton Abbot Devon

Contents

Illustrations   7

Publisher's Introduction   11

Chapter 1   Organisation, policy and practice   15

Chapter 2   Press advertising, letterpress posters and handbills   41

Chapter 3   Pictorial posters, folders and booklets   65

Chapter 4   Sale publications   83

Chapter 5   *Holiday Haunts*   104

Chapter 6   Miscellaneous forms of publicity   122

Chapter 7   The *Great Western Railway Magazine*   161

Appendix 1   Check list of sale publications   171

Appendix 2   Check list of jig-saw puzzles   183

Appendix 3   Check list of lantern slide lectures   185

Appendix 4   Check list of official postcards   186

Acknowledgements   197

Notes on sources   199

Index   203

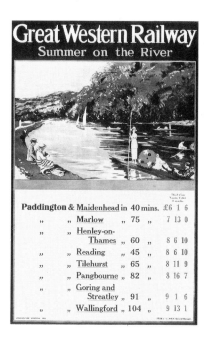

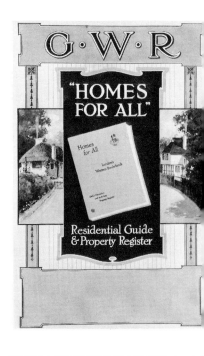

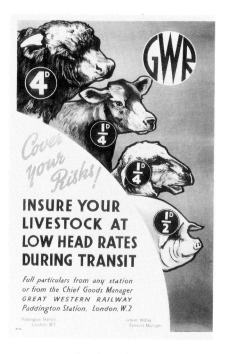

Four interesting posters portraying the different typography of GWR Poster Art

Illustrations

PLATES

Front page of the June 1865, Great Western Timetable   *frontispiece*

                                                                        Page

Four posters portraying different typography of GWR Poster Art   6
Two Swindon Works booklet covers; 1935 and 1947   10
Two posters. Air Fares Reductions and *Holiday Haunts*   14
Excursion programme, 1878   17
Bristol excursion programme, 1899   17
The earliest known pictorial poster, 1897 (*British Railways Western Region*)   17
Road Motor poster, *c* 1908 (*British Railways Western Region*)   17
Six pictorial posters, *c* 1908   18
Poster art at its worst, 1923   35
A popular poster of 1924 (*British Railways Western Region*)   35
Restaurant car poster, 1923 (*British Railways Western Region*)   35
Frank Newbould poster, 1936 (*British Railways Western Region*)   35
Saltash bridge poster, 1931 (*British Railways Western Region*)   36
Centenary poster, 1935 (*British Railways Western Region*)   36
Three early pictorial folders, *c* 1912   53
Pictorial folders, 1926-39   53
Camping coach booklet, 1934   54
Coronation tours booklet, 1937   54
Booklet for visit of *King George V* to America, 1927   54
Camping holidays booklet, 1934   54
The Engine Book, 1911-46   71
W. G. Chapman's first book, 1923   71
Typical cover of the *Rambles* series, 1938   71
Cover of *The Cornish Riviera*, 1934   72
Standard cover for A. M. Broadley's books   72
The Cornish Riviera, 1928   72
Chapter opening from *Cathedrals*, 1924   89
The first issue of *Holiday Haunts*, 1906   90
Holiday Haunts cover, 1911-28   90

Holiday Haunts cover, 1932   90
Holiday Haunts bookmarkers   90
Advertising motor car, 1907 (*British Railways Western Region*)   107
Picture postcard, 1904   107
Cheltenham Flyer jig-saw puzzle   108
Early pattern of jig-saw puzzle box   125
Later type of book box   125
Homes for All (Birmingham), 1913   126
Coloured luggage labels   143
Changing presentation of the GWR *Magazine*   144

IN THE TEXT

Excursion advertisement, 1862   15
Guide-book advertisement, 1878   20
Title-page of Wyld's guide, 1839   21
Title-page of Measom's guide, 1860   23
'Holiday Line' slogan, 1908   24
GWR emblem, 1914   26
'Go Great Western' emblems   27
Neo-post letter franking, 1926   28
Early form of roundel, 1912   32
The familiar roundel, 1934   32
Heath Robinson's *Railway Ribaldry*, 1935   33
Illustration from *Next Station*, 1947   39
Press advertisement, 1939   44
Small bill, 1878   52
Handbills of 1879, 1884, 1892, 1908, 1929 and
   1935   55, 56, 57, 58, 59, 60
Tourist Programme covers   61
Letterpress poster, 1902   62
Standard letterpress bills, 1922   63
Letterpress poster, 1939   64
Handbook for Travellers from Over Seas, 1912   77
Hiker's Mystery express leaflet, 1932   79
Advertisement for publications, 1912   85
Chapter opening from *Cheltenham Flyer*, 1934   92
'Handy Aids' series, title-page   93

Welsh Mountain Railways, 1924   94
Map from *Through the Window*, 1924   97
Chapter opening from *Somerset*, 1934   100
Folder for 'Boys of all Ages' series, *c* 1938   103
Announcement in *Holiday Haunts*, 1906   110
Holiday Haunts title-page, 1911-31   117
Title-page of centenary *Holiday Haunts*, 1935   119
Holiday Haunts advertisement   120
Lantern lecture booklets, *c* 1934 and 1947   123
Advertisement for carriage pictures, 1907   146
Souvenir luggage label, 1931   153
Advertisement for *Great Western Magazine*   170
Advertisement for 'Pictorial Post Cards'   186
Series 5 Postcard   191

Two covers of booklets on Swindon works. (left) *This publication issued in 1935; its 56 pages printed beautifully by Kelly and Kelly London; and* (right) *this 64 page booklet printed by Waterlow & Sons in 1947 and issued with a large pullout map of the works.* (see page 154)

Publisher's Introduction

Go Great Western! An evocative phrase: chocolate-and-cream coaches, a succession of famous locomotive classes all outwardly in the same tradition with green tapering boilers and shining brasswork; famous holiday expresses, slip coaches, lower-quadrant signals; pannier tanks drawing trains into a spotlessly-clean Paddington station, and 0–4–2 tanks for ever pausing for drinks at branch-line stations in idyllic situations well away from the towns and villages bearing their names . . . but above all a railway that was proud of itself, that cultivated its own way of life, different from the rest, anxious to impress itself, its staff and the public with its consequence and its mystique.

The GWR became a legend almost in its own lifetime. It was a distinction to live on it and travel by it, to have shares in it, read its annual reports or its *Holiday Haunts*, eat its Great Western assorted biscuits in the restaurant car, drink its own brand of whisky.

How did it all happen?

The company began, I suppose, in a curiously negative way, as a very conservative line, hating innovation, clinging to the proven, haughty, unambitious to serve its territory well. It was once extremely unpopular: Plymouth gave the arrival of the rival narrow gauge LSWR a far greater welcome than it had offered the very first trains on Brunel's broad gauge many years before. It was of course largely the broad gauge that delayed progress, and a great awakening followed its final abolition in the early 1890s. By 1914 the GWR had become a thoroughly efficient and energetically-managed line, though still nervous of innovation in some respects.

11

Then came the war and its troubled aftermath, and the 1923 'grouping' of Britain's main railways into four. Of these, three were new concoctions of groups of companies; only the GWR preserved its identity. Albeit the GWR absorbed some other lines, including the Cambrian Railways, essentially it remained the same —the same territory, trains and policy. It alone had the old-world 'Great' left in its title. This permanence, coupled with the reappearance of the chocolate-and-cream livery after an absence of some years, had an inevitable appeal in a changing world of motor cars, aeroplanes and industrial strife.

But it was not so much the railway's character as the way in which it was exploited that made the GWR so different, so famous. The management at Paddington understood the public's mood, books for 'Boys of all Ages' and the rest pouring forth from the press. Some of these publications had of course made their first appearance well before the first world war: the GWR always tended to be publicity-conscious, to do more to boost the growth of holiday resorts on its territory, than other railways. But it was only after 1923, and especially in the 1930s, that the company became a major publisher in its own right. Even those who think they remember what happened, or have a collection of GWR publications still on their shelves, will be surprised to see from Mr Wilson's text and appendix just how ambitious was the publications programme. No commercial organisation before or since has been so effective a publisher on so wide a front; jig-saw puzzles, films, books and other items, dealing with many subjects beside the railway.

The real achievement was the enormous interest created in the GWR itself. Everyone knew when the *Cornish Riviera Express* left Paddington, how the 'Kings' were an improvement on the 'Castles', exactly where along the route to see the Westbury white horse and the best glimpse of Dartmoor, how the *Cheltenham Flyer* became the world's fastest train. Star drivers became as well-known among schoolboys as today's pop idols; and the Cornish Riviera and Glorious Devon illusions were finally cemented.

Today much of the publicity material strikes us as raw, unsophisticated, not always even accurate. Looking back, too, one wonders whether the railway really was Great; the best trains may have been world-famous, but there were not many of them, and few would welcome a return to pre-war standards of seating comfort, leave alone pre-war schedules. In a sense the whole thing was an illusion as much as the Cornish Riviera and Glorious Devon. Yet the railway was tangibly colourful, permanent, proud, far more successful than the other three companies of the grouping era, and in its day and age the publicity must have added greatly to traffic and prestige.

Primarily this book will appeal to the enthusiast still bathing in the glory of the GWR—and it is after all only a decade since a chocolate-and-cream *Cornish Riviera Express* still left Paddington at 10.30 behind a 'King', non-stop for Plymouth. Tradition did not immediately halt with nationalisation. But this is also a work that should be read by those responsible for publicising modern industry, for there must still be some lessons to be learnt from the GWR's skilful use of public sentiment.

David St John Thomas

INTRODUCTION TO THE SECOND EDITION, 1987

Seventeen years have already elapsed since this work was first published, and many years now since its author died. What memories of visiting him in his bookshop near the top of Cheltenham's Parade, where there was always a fascinating array, not only of railway literature, but Great Western artifacts. Roger Burdett Wilson would have liked nothing better than to think his work carried on, and indeed this remains the standard book on a subject attracting greater rather than declining interest, as it becomes more widely recognised just how extraordinary the Great Western was in the wide spectrum of its publicity activities.

Colin Judge has kindly provided extra material for this book, and we are also indebted to Picton Publishing (Chippenham) Ltd for permission to reproduce post card details from *Official Railway Postcards of the British Isles*.

Enjoy going Great Western once more!

David St John Thomas

A 1926 poster advertising the popularity of Holiday Haunts

Reduction in Air Fares poster of 1933

Chapter 1

Organisation, Policy and Practice

The advertising policy of the railway companies during the nineteenth century was dictated by the virtual monopoly which they held in the transport of passengers and goods over all but the shortest distances. They were content to provide time and fare tables for regular services, to announce excursions and cheap trips, and to give notice of the opening of new stations and lines. Only in the last decade of the Victorian era did they begin to exploit the vast possibilities of wider and more subtle forms of advertising,

GREAT WESTERN RAILWAY.

INTERNATIONAL EXHIBITION.

CHEAP EXCURSION TRAIN
TO
LONDON.

ON MONDAY, JULY 7, 1862,

AN EXCURSION TRAIN will leave Hereford at 7.45 a.m., Ross 8.5 a.m., Cheltenham, 8.40 a.m., Gloucester, 9.0. a.m., arriving at Paddington at 1.45 p.m.; and will return from Paddington on Friday, July 11, and Tuesday, July 15, at 2.15 p.m.

The G. W. R. Station is one mile from the Exhibition.

Fares for the Double Journey:

	First Class.		Closed Car.
Cheltenham and Gloucester ...	14s.	...	7s.
Hereford and Ross	16s.	...	8s.

A Single Package of Luggage allowed.

Bristol, June 27th, 1862.

Excursion advertisement in the *Cheltenham Examiner,*
2 July 1862

mainly with a view to attracting holiday traffic, then developing rapidly as more and more families became able to enjoy a week at the seaside.

Such innovations as pictorial posters, illustrated literature and guides to holiday accommodation made their appearance in the 1890s and developed steadily after the turn of the century. But the lethargy bred of years of railway supremacy lingered on for a long time, and the railways were very slow to meet the increasing road competition after the first world war with anything like an adequate advertising campaign.

From the earliest days of the Great Western Railway the train services were brought to the notice of the public mainly through advertisements in London and provincial newspapers, by time books sold at station booking offices, and by letterpress bills displayed at stations. With the great increase in touring and travelling for pleasure which the railways facilitated, and indeed largely created, the Great Western, like other companies, advertised in the more popular series of guide books which appeared in almost annual editions from the 1860s.

In the company's early years there were also several guide books to the line itself, as there were to most of the early railways. In 1839, when the embryo Great Western had only reached Twyford, James Wyld's *Guide* and another (believed to be by G. T. Clark), were published, and Arthur Freeling's *Great Western Companion* followed a year later. In 1841, when London and Bristol were finally linked, Edward Mogg, who only nine years before had produced the last of the long line of Paterson's road books of the coaching age, published the first edition of his *Great Western Railway and Windsor, Bath and Bristol Guide*.

This publicity cost the company nothing, and it helped to popularise railway travel, particularly among the middle and upper classes of Victorian society. The Great Western was also fortunate in having the beautiful lithographs of J. C. Bourne, published in 1846, to create public interest in its scenery and engineering works. These early guides were followed twenty years later by the first of George Measom's massive *Official Guides* (1860) which ran to over 800 pages. Though called official, and dedicated, with permission, to the chairman and directors, it was,

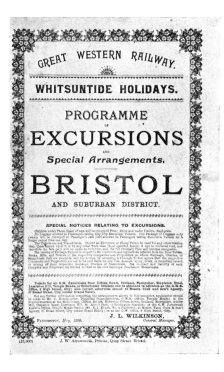

Page 17 (above left) *Excursion programme, 1878. Printed on mauve paper for binding with the penny time book;* (right) *Bristol excursion programme, 1899, pleasantly printed by Arrowsmith of Bristol on pink paper:* (below left) *the earliest known pictorial poster, 1897;* (right) *road motor poster c 1908*

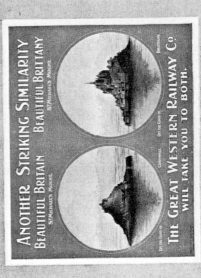

like its predecessors, produced entirely by the publisher, in this case Richard Griffin & Co. With its 350 engravings and over 200 pages of fascinating advertisements, it was exceedingly good value at a shilling a copy, bound in gilt-decorated cloth. Cassell & Co issued a series of official guides for the major railway companies, of which the Great Western volume first appeared in 1884. This ran into many editions until the series was discontinued soon after the first world war. Though not on the scale of Measom's immense tome, Cassell's *Guide* was based on information supplied by the company, and was regularly advertised in the penny time book.

These guide books were mainly topographical, and were not intended to supply information about train services; this most important part of the company's advertising was conducted mainly through the press. This policy became so firmly established during the early years that it took precedence over all other forms of publicity throughout the company's existence.

The Great Western used the services of an advertising agent at one period, but this practice was discontinued well before 1870. A brief undated report of about this time states that advertising was then done at the general manager's office and that the money saved on the agent's commission more than covered the wages of the clerk and cost of stationery and postage. The report went on to point out that all the large companies had bill inspectors, whose duty was to travel round the system and see that bills were properly displayed. It strongly recommended that two inspectors should be appointed on the Great Western, and a short list of nineteen candidates was appended. Of these, a Great Western guard named Lloyd, said by his superintendent to be 'an active, smart man', and an outside man with billposting experience, were given the jobs —at 35s and 27s (£1.75 and £1.35) per week.

The organisation of distribution of bills and time books had evidently been a very haphazard affair up to that time, and it was then to become the responsibility of the advertising clerk 'who will probably require the assistance of a youth'.

Advertisements for London papers and national periodicals and guide books were compiled at Paddington, but there was some delegation of authority to divisional offices in the case of local newspapers. It is apparent from the imprints on many handbills

B

Great Western Railway.

TOURIST ARRANGEMENTS, 1878.

First, Second, and Third Class Tourist Tickets, available for Two Months, and renewable on payment of a per centage up to December 31st, will be issued until October 31st, inclusive, at the Principal Stations on this Railway, to all the Watering and other places of attraction in the West of England, including:—

Clevedon	Ilfracombe	Torquay	Penzance
Weston-Super-Mare	Exeter	Plymouth	Dorchester
Minehead	Dawlish	Truro	Bridport
Barnstaple	Teignmouth	Falmouth	Weymouth and Channel Islands

To North and South Wales, including—

Dolgelley	Rhyl	Holyhead	Tenby
Barmouth	Llandudno	Chepstow	Pembroke
Aberystwith	Penmaenmawr	Swansea	New Milford

To Buxton	Windermere	Scarborough	Scotland
Matlock	Isle of Man	Whitby	

To Brighton	St. Leonards	Isle of Wight	Margate
Eastbourne	Hastings	Ramsgate	Dover

And to Waterford, Cork, Lakes of Killarney, Dublin, &c.

Passengers holding First or Second Class Tourist Tickets to the principal stations in the West of England can travel by the 11·45 a.m. Express Train from Paddington, which reaches Exeter in *four hours and a quarter*, and Plymouth in *six hours and a quarter*.

For particulars of the various Circular Tours, Fares, and other information, see the Company's Tourist Programmes, which can be obtained at the Stations and Booking-offices.

PIC-NIC AND PLEASURE PARTIES.

During the Summer months (until October 31st inclusive), First, Second, and Third Class Return Tickets, available for one day only, will be issued (with certain exceptions and limitations) at reduced fares, at all the principal Stations, to parties of not less than six first class or ten second or third class passengers.

To obtain these Tickets application must be made to one of the persons named below not less than three days before, giving full particulars of the proposed excursion.

EXCURSION TRAINS

At low fares will run at intervals during the season, to and from London, Liverpool, Manchester, Birmingham, Bristol, Worcester, Weymouth, the West of England, North and South Wales, the South of Ireland, and all parts of the Great Western system.

Full information as to Trains, Fares, Routes, &c., will be duly announced, and may be obtained on application to the Company's Superintendents: Mr. H. Hughes and Mr. A, Higgins, Paddington; Mr. H. Stevens, Reading ; Mr. T. Graham or Mr. T. W. Walton, Bristol; Mr. C. E. Compton, Plymouth; Mr. J. Richardson, Par ; Mr. G. S. Denbigh, Penzance ; Mr. G.C. Grover, Hereford; Mr. J. Kelley, Chester, Mr. N. J. Burlinson, Birmingham ; Mr. H. Y. Adye, Worcester; Mr. T. I. Allen, Newport (Mon.); Mr. H. Besant, Swansea; and Mr. P. Donaldson, Pontypool Road (Mon.).

J. GRIERSON, General Manager.

Paddington Terminus.

Full-page advertisement in *Gossiping Guide to Wales*, 1878

THE

GREAT WESTERN,

CHELTENHAM AND GREAT WESTERN,

AND

BRISTOL AND EXETER

RAILWAY GUIDES:

CONTAINING

A TOPOGRAPHICAL, ANTIQUARIAN, AND GEOLOGICAL ACCOUNT
OF THE COUNTRY, AND OF THE TOWNS AND VILLAGES
IN THE NEIGHBOURHOOD OF THE RAILWAYS:

WITH A

PRELIMINARY DESCRIPTION

OF THE

CONSTRUCTION OF THE GREAT WESTERN AND
OTHER RAILWAYS,

ILLUSTRATED WITH

NUMEROUS AND ACCURATE ENGRAVINGS ON WOOD;

AND

GUIDES

TO

Windsor, Reading, Oxford, Glocester, Hereford,
Cheltenham, Bath, Wells, and Bristol.

LONDON:

PUBLISHED BY JAMES WYLD,

GEOGRAPHER TO THE QUEEN,

CHARING-CROSS, EAST, FOUR DOORS FROM TRAFALGAR-SQUARE.

1839.

Title-page of James Wyld's guide of 1839

and letterpress posters of the 1880s that these were printed under
divisional arrangements by local firms. The overall supervision
of advertising was in the hands of the general manager's office,
but the Great Western was nearly half a century old before a
separate advertising office was thought necessary.

It was in 1886, near the close of James Grierson's long and
distinguished career as general manager, that the importance of
advertising began to be appreciated, and an advertising department
formed in the general manager's office. It was a modest beginning,

with a staff of no more than half a dozen clerks. The department inherited policies and methods which had changed little for decades, policies which typifed the conservatism and lack of enterprise of G. N. Tyrrell's years as the first superintendent of the line. But the Great Western was on the threshold of better times. In 1888 Tyrrell was succeeded by N. J. Burlinson and in April 1894, when he was followed by T. I. Allen, the advertising department was transferred from the general manager's office to the traffic side under the superintendent of the line. Although it was some time before the new arrangements bore fruit, the organisation was established and was ready to play its part in the resurgence of Great Western prosperity and prestige which was soon to come under the triumvirate which managed the company's affairs in the later 1890s—Viscount Emlyn (chairman), Joseph Wilkinson (general manager) and T. I. Allen (superintendent of the line).

Advertising matter, by its very nature, is ephemeral and usually destroyed once its purpose has been served. No complete collection of Great Western publicity exists among the company's surviving archives, and the publicity output of many other companies is barely represented at all in official collections, so that it is by no means easy to discern trends in style and content, and still less to make a detailed comparison between the publicity of the various railways. It can, however, be said that in the nineteenth century there was little to choose between one company and another. Little or no attention seems to have been paid to design or layout, and in any case letterpress posters, handbills, and press advertisements were usually left to the discretion, or lack of it, of the printer's compositor. Throughout the history of railways the companies copied one another's ideas, not the least in advertising, and it is interesting to note a minute of a superintendents' meeting of 16 October 1884, where a letter from the general manager, James Grierson, was read, and 'Superintendents were directed to send to the office of the Superintendent of the Line copies of every Guide, Notice and Pamphlet issued by competing Companies or otherwise . . . from which hints and information could be obtained'.

Throughout the latter part of the nineteenth and well into the twentieth century, the principal means of direct contact with the prospective passenger was the printed handbill. Booking halls,

THE OFFICIAL
ILLUSTRATED GUIDE
TO THE
GREAT WESTERN RAILWAY,

INCLUDING

THE OXFORD, WORCESTER AND WOLVERHAMPTON,

AND

CHESTER AND HOLYHEAD LINES,
AND ISLE OF MAN.

WITH DESCRIPTIONS OF THE MOST

Important Manufactories in the Several Towns on the Lines.

BY GEORGE MEASOM,

AUTHOR OF THE OFFICIAL ILLUSTRATED GUIDES TO THE
NORTH WESTERN, GREAT NORTHERN, BRIGHTON, SOUTH WESTERN, SOUTH EASTERN,
CALEDONIAN, LANCASTER AND CARLISLE, EDINBURGH AND GLASGOW,
BRISTOL AND EXETER, SOUTH DEVON, SOUTH WALES, CORNWALL,
AND NORTHERN OF FRANCE, RAILWAYS.

EMBELLISHED WITH 350 ENGRAVINGS.

LONDON:

Published under the Special Authority of the Directors, by

RICHARD GRIFFIN AND CO.,

STATIONERS' HALL COURT;

AND SOLD BY THE PRINCIPAL BOOKSELLERS IN THE SEVERAL TOWNS ON
THE LINES, AND AT ALL THE RAILWAY STATIONS.

ONE SHILLING.

Title-page of Measom's guide, 1860

offices and Thomas Cook's travel agencies were festooned with multi-coloured bunches of bills offering cheap trips and excursions to seaside and inland resorts, sporting events and exhibitions, and to London and provincial towns.

By the 70s the Great Western was issuing comprehensive Tourist Arrangements consisting of twenty or more closely printed pages of fares for 'pic-nic or pleasure parties', available during the summer months. These were printed in folio format so that they could be bound in at the beginning of the penny time book as well as issued separately. By the 90s these had evolved into the Season Programme of Excursion Arrangements, printed in a smaller format, the pages of which looked much like a series of handbills, and before the turn of the century these had acquired a few pages of descriptive notes on the 'principal places of attraction'.

Here we see the beginning of the company's campaign to attract holiday traffic to the line by exploiting the fact that it served so many resorts in Somerset, Devon and Cornwall, and in Wales. This was to bring enormous benefits to a railway which began with the great disadvantage that it included so few large towns and industrial areas in its routes. In the years that lay ahead tourist traffic to the West Country and the Welsh coast brought a welcome addition to the company's passenger revenue. The slogan 'The Holiday Line' suggested by Archibald Edwards, a South Wales artist, adopted by the Great Western in 1908, was to prove both apt and rewarding.

G.W.R.–The Holiday Line

'The Holiday Line' slogan as it first appeared in *Holiday Haunts* for 1908

It was in the 1890s that a London publisher, Walter Hill, produced for several railway companies a series of booklets giving general information on holiday resorts and detailed lists of hotels and other accommodation. The Great Western volume first appeared in 1894 and new editions were published annually until

1905, when it had grown to over 200 pages, with a good number of half-tone illustrations and a large map. Its full title was *Great Western Railway: Farmhouse, Seaside, Country Lodgings, Boarding Houses & Hotels*. It was evidently so successful that in 1906 the company's advertising department produced its own book on similar lines, though much enlarged and with elaborately printed stiff covers. The long-winded title was jettisoned in favour of one more easily remembered—a title, indeed, which is still remembered today by countless old Great Western passengers—*Holiday Haunts*.

In January 1904 the sudden death of Sir Joseph Wilkinson brought the Chief Engineer, James C. Inglis, to Paddington as general manager. While some of the developments which bore fruit during his regime had been initiated under his predecessor, a good deal of the Great Western's increasing prestige during the early years of the new century was due to his progressive policy and energetic management, and this is especially true in the field of publicity. Although the progress in the post-war period under Felix Pole, and particularly the contribution of W. H. Fraser as publicity agent, must not be underrated, it is nevertheless true that the real foundations of modern Great Western publicity were laid in Inglis' time.

Of the many innovations in the publicity field at this time perhaps the most important was the publication of the first of a long series of travel books which were to bring much prestige, and doubtless additional traffic, to the Great Western during the next forty years. Early in 1904 a handsome book of 152 pages, with illustrations and a map, made its appearance on the bookstalls. The stylish white card cover bore the title *The Cornish Riviera* and the coat of arms of the GWR in gold. Modestly priced at three-pence, this book was an historic volume for two reasons: it was the first of all the Great Western books, and on its cover the now familiar words Cornish Riviera appeared for the first time. *The Cornish Riviera* and its successors set a high standard of design and production unequalled in railway literature. (A fuller account of these sale publications is given in Chapter 4.) Though the Great Western had its imitators, particularly after the grouping of 1923, no other company produced anything near the output of these immensely popular books. Their popularity may be measured both by the sales figures (so far as they have survived) and by the regularity with which, even today, they appear in second-hand bookshops, to be bought again and relished by a generation to whom they are a tangible memorial to the enterprise of the Great Western.

The novel idea of asking the public to pay for what was, after all, publicity, was further developed in later years. One of the most successful schemes was the issue of jig-saw puzzles in the 1920s and 30s, through which the younger generation was introduced discreetly to the magnificence of Great Western locomotives and to the charms of the scenery along The Holiday Line.

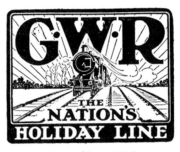

GWR emblem, 1914

Alongside this publishing activity the advertising department set about its task in many other ways. Press advertising continued as the mainstay, linked with posters and handbills. The company had enquiry offices at agricultural shows and stands at the larger exhibitions. As early as 1906, only three years after the commencement of the pioneer motor omnibus service between Helston and the Lizard, the Great Western was advertising the Cornish Riviera and its train services through special buses adapted as mobile poster hoardings which went on extensive tours of the country. Road motors, to use the official term, also featured in some of the earliest pictorial folders, which had begun to appear in increasing numbers by 1910, and which developed greatly in the inter-war years; by 1938 some three-quarters of a million folders were being distributed in a single year. Cheaper and better methods of colour printing were exploited to the full and by the mid-1930s Great Western folders had reached a high standard of design.

Coloured pictorial posters were another step forward taken in the 1890s. A four-colour poster for Ascot race trains, dated June 1897, is displayed in the Great Western Railway Museum at Swindon, and is said to be the earliest surviving example.

A considerable part of the advertising department's work was centred on a succession of slogans and campaigns which are clearly discernible in surviving publicity material. Before the first world war, in addition to 'The Holiday Line' and 'The Cornish Riviera', there was a campaign to encourage the 'week-end habit'. In the

Go Great Western emblem, 1923

1920s the slogan 'Go Great Western' appeared in books and folders, and even glass inkwells incorporating the slogan were produced. National campaigns like the 'Come to Britain' movement of the late 20s and the 'Buy British' campaign of the depressed 1930s were reflected in Great Western advertising, as were the 'Earlier Holidays' campaigns of the later 20s and 30s.

In 1934 the public was being reminded that it was 'Quicker by Rail'—a slogan taken up by all the railway companies as an antidote to the rapidly developing congestion on the roads. Road accidents were also rising in number, and it was suggested the railways should adopt the slogan 'It's Safer and Quicker by Rail'. This was well borne out by the fact that only one passenger had been killed on the GWR between 1916 and 1934—but railwaymen were superstitious and safety as an advertising feature was taboo with all railways.

Go Great Western emblem, 1926

It is ironical that the last of these campaigns was the extensive publicity appeal for a 'Fair Deal for the Railways' launched by the four group companies in November 1938, in an effort to persuade the government to repeal the regulations governing freight charges which had for so long hampered the economic progress of the railways. The war came before any action had been taken, and with it came government control and an almost complete cessation of railway publicity.

The appointment in 1921 of Felix J. C. Pole as general manager, at the early age of 44, came at a crucial time in the company's affairs, with the frustration and restrictions of the war barely over and the implementation of the Railways Act of 1921 less than two years away. Pole was keenly aware of the value of good and effective publicity, and had experience in railway journalism as editor of the *Great Western Railway Magazine* from 1909 to 1919, and as a writer on railway topics in the press. It seems difficult to believe that Sir Felix Pole's term of office as general manager only lasted eight years, for his name appears on the title-

Neo-post letter franking, 1926

page of so many of the company's publications during the golden age of Great Western publicity.

Pole threw himself into his new job with tremendous energy, not a little of which was reserved for publicity and what he called propaganda. This was nothing more or less than the familiar public relations of our own day. Pole not only wrote articles for the press, but encouraged other members of the staff to do likewise, and he frequently addressed Chambers of Commerce and business clubs throughout the country, and some of his speeches were reprinted in pamphlet form for free distribution in business and commercial circles.

In his memoirs, Sir Felix Pole described the advertising department in 1921 as highly efficient, but wartime restrictions had stunted its growth and a fresh move forward was clearly necessary in the challenging period which was to come as the railways regained their independence and traffic returned to normal after the war.

It was, however, something like three years before two important steps were taken to provide the Great Western with a sufficiently strong publicity arm to meet the needs of a go-ahead railway in the post-grouping era.

The grouping of 1923 had little immediate effect on the scope of the company's publicity. The South Wales companies which came into the GWR fold, being mainly goods and mineral lines, added little or nothing to the company's holiday attractions; the reverse, however, was true of the Cambrian Railways, but as that company's publicity was already well developed as a direct result of its dependence on passenger traffic, the GWR was able to adapt this to its own needs. As early as 1909 a Cambrian Resorts Association had been formed under Cambrian Railways auspices, and this continued to operate in Great Western days, with H. Warwick (formerly superintendent of the line of the Cambrian, later district traffic manager at Oswestry) as its secretary. Another former Cambrian man, H. Browning Button, who was taken onto the publicity staff at Paddington after the grouping, was sent back to Oswestry to co-ordinate publicity in North and Central Wales.

In 1924 the advertising department in the superintendent of the line's office was enlarged and given the title of publicity department, though it was still under the direct control of the superintendent of the line's office and was not given the independence enjoyed by the stationery and printing department. As head of the new department, with the title of publicity agent, Pole appointed William Henry Fraser. Fraser had been with the GWR since 1892 and had served in a number of departments, gaining the wide experience and knowledge of railway matters essential to his new post.

The choice of Fraser for this important job was an inspired one. A man of great personal charm and integrity, he was full of ideas and a splendid organiser. He not only initiated many improvements in Great Western publicity, but also quickly gained the confidence of the press, for whom he arranged many special visits to Great Western territory. Journalism was in his blood—his brother Lovat Fraser had been editor of the *Times of India* and leader-writer on *The Times*, and his daughter was later to be very closely associated with the GWR. Fraser, incidentally, bore a strong physical resemblance to Sir Felix Pole, and in the corridors at Paddington he was often mistaken for the general manager, sometimes with amusing results.

During his years as publicity agent the company's publicity made great strides, and many highly successful schemes were carried through during this eventful period. The sale publications went from strength to strength, with the books in W. G. Chapman's 'For Boys of all Ages' series, the beautifully produced *Cathedrals, Abbeys* and *Castles*, and the books by S. P. B. Mais on the ever-topical subjects of Devon and Cornwall. The steady increase in the size and printings of *Holiday Haunts* was one of the greatest achievements of the department in Fraser's time, the sales rising from 100,000 copies of 712 pages in 1924 to 200,000 copies of 964 pages in 1928.

The sale publications were not the only indirect method of publicity adopted successfully. W. H. Fraser carried through an extended programme of liaison with holiday towns, whereby the company and local authorities shared the cost of publicising the resorts. Here the emphasis was on attracting holidaymakers to specific places on the Great Western system, and since the great majority still, at that time, travelled by rail rather than by road, the Great Western automatically reaped the benefit. This policy was carried into press advertising as well as in posters and folders, and special press visits were arranged by the GWR to coastal towns like Torquay, St Ives and Aberystwyth, as well as to Bath, Stratford-upon-Avon and other inland resorts. When the International Hotel Alliance visited Britain in 1926 the Great Western ran a special train to Oxford and Stratford and supplied an illustrated souvenir booklet for the guests.

In the 1930s the increasing competition from road transport, both for passengers and goods, brought the four group companies closer together than at any previous time, and joint publicity schemes with the LMS and Southern companies were instituted during Fraser's regime. In 1925 Fraser was sent to the United States and Canada to improve relations with the travelling public and business firms, and in January of that year a special 72-page booklet was issued as a *Handbook for Travellers from Overseas*.

When Fraser retired at the end of 1931 after forty years with the GWR he left a vigorous and up-to-date publicity department which was playing its full part in persuading the travelling public to 'Go Great Western'. On his retirement the *Magazine* said of him, 'Mr Fraser is probably one of the best known men not only on the Company's system, but at all the holiday resorts, seaside and inland, between Weymouth and Aberystwyth'.

W.. H. Fraser was succeeded by K. W. C. Grand, who from 1926 to 1929 had been the GWR general agent in the United States and Canada. On his return to Paddington he was appointed assistant to Fraser and in January 1931 became the first head of a new department controlling commercial advertising on the Great Western. From 1 January 1932 Grand combined this latter post with that of publicity agent. K. W. C. Grand had joined the company in 1919 and served under the divisional superintendent at Paddington before going to the general manager's office in 1922. He was destined to be the first chief regional officer after nationalisation, seeing his old company through the difficult period of transition after 1 January 1948.

Up to this time the company's publicity matter had incorporated either the full GREAT WESTERN RAILWAY or the initials GWR, sometimes with the addition of the coat of arms. Grand felt that something more modern was needed by which the public could recognise Great Western publicity at a glance. The idea bore fruit in the now familiar roundel monogram, which was designed by Arthur Sawyer, head of production in the publicity department. One of the first appearances of the new symbol was on an illustrated folder advertising the Lleyn Peninsula which was issued in June 1931. Thereafter it was incorporated in an increasing number of folders, posters and other matter, and in the summer of 1934 it was adopted for Great Western rolling stock and uniforms. The basic idea was by no means new; a primitive form of the monogram had been used in a press advertisement, and possibly elsewhere, at least as early as 1912.

In July 1933, on Grand's appointment as commercial assistant to the superintendent of the line, G. E. Orton, another Great Western man with considerable experience in publicity, became the new agent. Orton had been with the GWR for thirty years, and was a junior in the old advertising department in 1903, afterwards going to the general manager's office. He succeeded K. W. C. Grand in America, returning in 1931 to be Grand's assistant in the publicity department. Like his predecessor, Orton became commercial assistant in the summer of 1934. At this time advertising and publicity were becoming increasingly specialised occupations, and it is not altogether surprising to find that when the post of publicity agent again became vacant on Orton's promotion, the new man was not a railwayman.

Early form of roundel monogram, in use in 1912

The roundel monogram brought into general use in 1934, as it appeared in the *Magazine* for September of that year

Major M. J. M. Dewar only joined the Great Western in October 1933, to take charge of the trade advertising department. His previous career, apart from service in the regular army, had been entirely in publicity. He was on the headquarters staff of the British Empire Exhibition at Wembley in 1924-5, and joined the Empire Marketing Board at its inception, spending seven years as head of its outdoor publicity. With this change at the head of the department at Paddington the appointment was renamed Publicity Officer.

Major Dewar took over at a time when the economic depression was beginning to recede and holiday traffic was resuming its

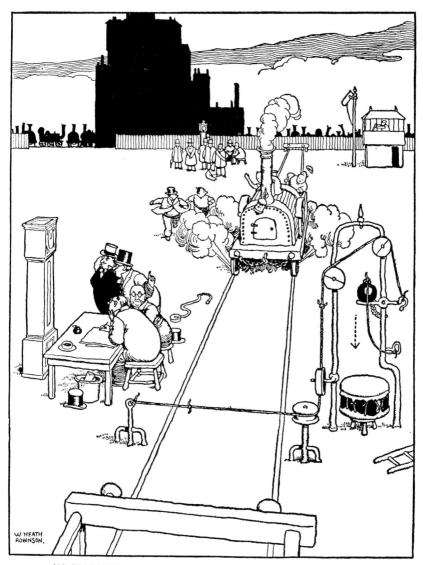

AN OLD-FASHIONED METHOD OF TESTING THE SPEED OF ENGINES

From W. Heath Robinson's *Railway Ribaldry,* 1935

importance. Sales of *Holiday Haunts* which had dropped by 25 per cent between 1931 and 1933, were increasing again, and some very attractive travel literature and posters were produced for the remaining few summer seasons before the second world war. The publicity department under Major Dewar was also occupied with a large-scale advertising campaign in co-operation with the other main-line companies and the Irish railways, with a special eye on American and Continental tourists. The monogram ABIR (Associated British and Irish Railways), similar in design to the new GWR roundel, appeared on much of the literature for this campaign, the production of which was undertaken by the Great Western. It is significant that the whole idea of joint publicity by the group companies was first suggested at the Railway Clearing House by the Great Western.

The principal event of this period, and one unique in British railway history, was the centenary of the Great Western Railway which was celebrated in 1935, and much work in connection with this important occasion naturally fell to the publicity department. It is disappointing to find that only one sale publication was produced for the event, and a light-hearted one at that—W. Heath Robinson's *Railway Ribaldry*, but a short illustrated history, reprinted from *The Times*, was produced for presentation, and elaborate souvenirs and menu cards were produced for the centenary banquets at Paddington and Bristol. The most ambitious part of the celebrations was the making of a centenary film depicting scenes in the history of the company and its current activities.

Travel publicity was intensifying in the late 1930s as prosperity returned. In 1936 two campaigns occupied the department's attention; another 'Come to Britain' movement was launched with an extended tour of this country by Continental travel agents and journalists and a dinner given by the Hotel Association, while for home consumption the railways launched a campaign to persuade families to take earlier holidays to reduce the congestion and pressure on railway facilities during the month of August. The following year brought the pageantry of the coronation of King George VI, for which many overseas visitors came to this country. Special tours were arranged and a large number of special trains

Footnote:- Two printings of *Railway Ribaldry* appeared. The title page of the second printing was inscribed with 'GWR May 1935'

Page 35 (above left) *Poster art at its worst, 1923;* (right) *a popular poster of 1924;* (below left) *restaurant car poster, 1923;* (right) *the colourful simplicity of Frank Newbould, 1936*

Page 36 (above) *Saltash bridge by Avan Anrooy, 1931;* (below) *M. Secretan's centenary poster, 1935*

and cheap bookings were provided to enable the public to see the procession in London and the festivities in provincial centres. All this meant additional publicity work which included the decoration of Paddington station and the London receiving offices.

The excitement of the coronation had hardly died away before the Munich crisis of 1938, and preparations began for the war which followed within a year. In 1939 there was the Empire Exhibition at Glasgow, at which the railway companies had a stand and enquiry office, and the Great Western produced a film for general release entitled *Cornwall—the Western Land*. The call of the west was used as well in a more sinister sense in a poster issued in 1939 to attract more industry to the West Country and South Wales, with more than a hint that the parts of Britain farthest from the Continent would be less vulnerable to air attack in the event of war.

With the outbreak of war almost all publicity work came to a standstill. As preparations were so far advanced it was possible to issue the 1940 edition of *Holiday Haunts*, though how many copies were sold is not recorded; by the time the glorious summer of 1940 arrived, Britain was too busy extricating its Expeditionary Force from France and preparing for Hitler's threatened invasion to give much thought to holidays.

Major Dewar was back in the army in February 1940, in the traditional railwayman's service, the Royal Engineers. After periods at Longmoor and other depots he was invalided from the service in December 1943 and returned to Paddington. During his absence George Dyall was appointed acting publicity officer. George Dyall had been chief clerk in the department since 1930 and had a long and valuable record of service to Great Western publicity, having joined the old advertising department as long ago as March 1897, in the stirring days of Wilkinson and T. I. Allen. Perhaps his most interesting job in his 45 years service was at the time of the grouping in 1923, when he was responsible for reorganising the publicity facilities at stations and offices on the newly acquired lines. He retired in 1942 and died in 1968. R. F. Hurford, the trade advertising agent, became acting publicity officer pending Major Dewar's return.

In 1943 W. H. Fraser, who might be called the father of the

C

modern Great Western publicity department, died at the age of 68. It was fitting that at the funeral service, which was attended by his successor K. W. C. Grand (then assistant general manager) and many of his former colleagues, the organ was played by George Orton. A year later the department lost another of its old staff, Charles Beaumont, who from 1930 to 1940 had been in charge of production of *Holiday Haunts* and pictorial posters. He had also represented the GWR on the Railway Clearing House joint publicity sub-committee, and on the ABIR American advertising sub-committee. He had been appointed editor of the *Magazine* in January 1943, and died in March 1944 as a result of injuries sustained during civil defence duty during an air raid. It is significant that Charles Beaumont, when still in the Goods Department at Plymouth in 1912, was one of many members of the staff who sent in suggestions as to how the company's publicity could be improved, and this may well have influenced his appointment in the following year to the advertising department at Paddington.

When peace returned in 1945, the railways, after six years of magnificent service under enormous difficulties, did their best to improve services and get rid of many of the tiresome restrictions of wartime, but the return to full peacetime services was clearly going to be a very slow and gradual process. Nevertheless, the GWR was looking ahead, and one of the company's first changes came in publicity policy, to bring it into line with trends which had developed during the war. The publicity department was transferred from the superintendent of the line's office back to the general manager's side, and G. E. Orton was given overall charge as chief officer for public relations, with Major Dewar as publicity officer and C. S. Lock, who had been head of the press section from 1927 to 1939, was appointed press officer.

Another change, involving some infusion of new blood from outside the company, came with the appointment as assistant to the chief officer of Christian Barman, an architect and industrial designer of outstanding ability. From 1935 to 1941 Barman was publicity officer to the London Passenger Transport Board, and during his term of office had greatly improved and modernised the visual presentation of London's transport system. He came to

Paddington after wartime service with the Ministry of Works as Assistant Director of Post-war Building.

One of Christian Barman's first publicity projects was to write a book outlining the Great Western Railway's post-war plans. This book, *Next Station—A Railway Plans for the Future,* was published for the company by Allen & Unwin Ltd in 1947, and the layout and coloured illustrations matched the fresh and vigorous approach by the company to problems of post-war transport. But the sands were running out. On the first page of the *Magazine* for October 1947 *Next Station* was reviewed, and alongside was an announcement with the heading Transport Act, 1947. Within three months the railways of Britain were vested in the British Transport Commission, and the destinies of the Great Western ceased to be guided by its board of directors as they had been for 112 years.

The light that had burned, always steadily, often with great brilliance, since 1835, was extinguished. Not unnaturally, many

A Great Western Gas Turbine locomotive preliminary design, 1946. Illustration from *Next Station,* 1947

of the chief officers retired at the end of the year, Sir James Milne, the general manager, and F. R. E. Davis, the company's secretary, among them. In the publicity department work went on much as usual, with Major Dewar continuing at its head. In 1949 he became the first public relations and publicity officer of the Western Region of British Railways. Major Dewar died in office on 23 November, 1952.

Chapter 2

Press Advertising, Letterpress Posters and Handbills

It may not be generally realised that press advertising was always regarded as the most important and effective form of railway publicity. From the announcement in *The Times* on 2 June 1838 of the opening of the Great Western Railway from Paddington to Maidenhead, the London and provincial newspapers remained the principal channel of communication between the company and the public. Even in 1925, by which time many other forms of publicity had been developed, G. E. Orton stated quite categorically that 'newspaper advertising I place first in importance every time'. He went on to say that press announcements usually went hand in hand with the issue of posters, with which he doubtless intended to include handbills.

The Times was already fifty years old when the first train ran into Maidenhead, and there were other, rival papers published in London, but in the provinces daily newspapers did not appear until 1855, the year in which the newspaper stamp duty was abolished. The repeal of the advertisement tax two years before had paved the way for an extension of advertising which was to play a considerable part in railway practice later in the century. But the railways themselves, and the electric telegraph (demonstrated so dramatically on the Great Western at Slough in 1845) both proved of enormous help in the development of the press, the latter facilitating the gathering of news and the former providing a means of rapid distribution of the papers.

In early Victorian England the newspapers carried a considerable amount of advertising matter devoted to transport of one sort or

another—railways, coastwise shipping, canal carrying and turn-
pike trusts. During the 'mania' *The Times* might carry more than
forty columns of railway promoters' advertisements. These were
not displayed, but set in types little or no larger than those used for
the editorial matter, much as auctioneers' announcements are
printed today in many provincial papers. There was, in fact, an
embargo on the use of large type in advertisements for many years,
but they were sometimes made more conspicuous by the inclusion
of a small engraving of a train or ship. These were printed from
stock blocks or metal types, and therefore bore no resemblance to
the rolling stock or vessels used by the advertiser. Some of the railway blocks, which in design clearly belonged to the late 1830s or
early 40s, were often still in use in the 60s or even 70s in provincial newspapers. A Great Western excursion announcement in *The
Cheltenham Examiner* for 2 July 1862 is headed by a train with a
guard seated on the roof of every carriage! (see page 15)

The Great Western, in common with other railway companies,
made extensive use of these small advertisements throughout the
nineteenth century and the first half of the twentieth, and the
great majority of the space was utilised for timetables or to
announce excursion trains, cheap fares and similar facilities. Little
attempt was made until comparatively recent times to inform the
public of the many ancillary services of the railway, and still less
was there any notion of propaganda or publicity as we know it
today. Although in later years critics of the railways often drew
attention to this, the companies had a ready answer: the only
practicable means of travel, or of goods transport, was by train,
and therefore any campaign like that used in the 1930s—'It's
Quicker by Rail'—was superfluous.

The increased activity in publicity which marked J. C. Inglis'
years as general manager of the Great Western (1903-11) was
reflected as much in press advertising as in other fields. In 1904
the company again resorted to the use of an advertising agent,
which it had discarded more than thirty years before. This time it
was Wills Ltd, of Cannon Street, whose work included the distribution of advertisements to the press as well as collecting them
for insertion in the early editions of the travel books and in
Holiday Haunts. Although this saved work at Paddington, it

naturally cost more, and after the first war the practice was again discontinued.

1904 saw the first real break with tradition when the company took a whole page in the *Daily Mail* for an illustrated advertisement. As the *Stocks and Shares Review* put it, 'old shareholders must have rubbed their eyes with astonishment at the sight of such a show of enterprise'. In succeeding years more use was made of displayed advertising, a good deal of which included reference to the appropriate sale publication, for which the public was invited to 'send 6d stamps to the Superintendent of the Line'. This had the dual purpose of selling the books (which themselves helped to sell railway tickets) and of giving the advertising department a useful guide to the effectiveness of the advertisements. A group of early displayed advertisements was illustrated in the *Magazine* in August 1910. Among the subjects covered were the Cornish Riviera, Ireland, North Wales, the current penny time book, and the Birmingham 2 hour expresses.

The smaller, non-displayed advertisements, inserted week after week in hundreds of local papers, usually in the same position so that readers would know where to find them, remained the backbone of Great Western press advertising, keeping the public informed of local excursions to the seaside, cheap trips to London and all the other tempting bargains which the railways had to offer. After the first war the Great Western was spending so much on press advertising that the company instituted a system of annual contracts with local papers, by which it agreed to take a given amount of space each year in return for reduced rates, and in doing so a very great saving was made. A proportion of the space was used for displayed matter, including publicity for *Holiday Haunts* and other publications.

There was a significant improvement in the style of display from 1927, and the impact on the public can be gauged from the response to an 'Earlier Holidays' press campaign in the following year which brought 12,000 letters from newspaper readers.

Even in the later years anything in the nature of market research was in its infancy, and a good deal of money, inevitably, was wasted. This was particularly true where more than one railway company advertised in the same area, and in national newspapers

The Charm of late August & September

SUMMER ATTRACTIONS STILL IN FULL SWING

WARMER SEAS

COMFORTABLE TRAVEL

TRAVEL BY RAIL

- **CHEAP MONTHLY RETURN TICKETS** available by any train, any day, are issued all the year round between most stations.

- **SEAT RESERVATION AND RESTAURANT CAR FACILITIES** on most Main Line Expresses.

- **LUGGAGE IN ADVANCE** saves expense & inconvenience

- **HOLIDAY SEASON or CONTRACT TICKETS** (issued up to October 31st) for a week's unlimited travel in selected areas at very cheap rates.

- **CIRCULAR TOURS** arranged from "anywhere to anywhere" in Great Britain at considerable saving in fares.

Enquire at any Railway Station, Office or Agency for all information

IT'S QUICKER BY RAIL !

Press advertisement, 1939

and periodicals. A realisation of this fact among the group companies led the Great Western to suggest, in 1929, that they should introduce joint advertising, and much of the publicity for 'Penny a Mile' fares and the 'It's Quicker by Rail' and other campaigns of the later 1930s was undertaken in this way.

By the 1930s the task of informing the public of cheap trips and excursions had assumed considerable proportions. There were something like 25,000 such trips annually, and notices of these trains appeared in about 250 newspapers each week, while as many as a quarter of a million letterpress posters and several million handbills were issued in a year. This entailed a great deal of planning and clerical work at Paddington, where a series of lists was kept showing the areas in which each paper circulated, so that the appropriate paper could be selected for each advertisement. Handbills, for which the copy was usually prepared in divisional offices, were printed by a local firm under the extra train notice contract, and advance proofs of these bills were sent to Paddington, from which the publicity department drafted the press announcement, which was then sent to the appropriate paper.

The increasing number of foreign visitors coming to Britain between the wars led the Great Western to advertise in German, Dutch and other continental papers, and, in co-operation with the Southern Railway, in the American press.

There is a familiar ring in the report of the publicity department for 1931, a year of extreme depression in trade. 'In view of the financial position of the country and the devaluation of the pound, with a consequent discouragement of travel to foreign resorts, special press advertising has been entered into with a view to directing public attention to the merits of the English "Riviera" . . .' The Cornish Riviera was still the Great Western's trump card.

The virtual monopoly in the transport of goods, held for so long by the railways, was at least partly responsible for the almost complete neglect of the subject in press advertising. It was only in the 1930s that, faced with increasing road competition, the Great Western began to allot some of its newspaper space to this important part of its traffic, and to advertise such services as country cartage and door-to-door containers.

Cost was always of paramount importance in considering advertising policy. Unlike manufacturers, who could put the cost of advertising onto the price of their goods, the railways, because of statutory control of rates, could not do likewise. The amount of money spent by the Great Western on advertising was, by present day standards, very small—in 1888 it was £5,952, and although it rose to £9,134 in 1898 it had dropped to only £6,781 in 1901.

The regular advertising contracts with newspapers placed the Great Western in a favourable position when it came to editorial coverage of important developments on the company's system and of the resorts it served. Railways were often in the news, though seldom in the headlines except when the rare accident occurred. Local railway matters were usually covered by the papers' reporters, and the GWR arranged for members of divisional staffs to contribute to their local newspapers, and to keep a watchful eye on the correspondence columns. But a great deal of propaganda for the Great Western was supplied by the publicity department in the form of articles. The GWR was the first railway company to establish a press bureau, and at one time was much envied by the other companies for the coverage it received in the press. An average of 200 news items was circulated annually, and as much as 4,000 column inches was devoted to important items of Great Western news such as the introduction of the diesel railcars and the Railway Air Services.

In the 1930s many of these articles were written by Maxwell Fraser, whose other work for the department is mentioned elsewhere. The extent of this important branch of publicity can be judged from the fact that the cuttings of Miss Fraser's articles fill three very large scrapbooks. With so much of the other publicity matter either lost or widely scattered in public or private collections, the files of national and local newspapers represent the only continuous record still extant of the Great Western's publicity during its long and unique life, and a detailed study and analysis would be a richly rewarding field for research.

Although national and local papers were the principal medium, the GWR, in common with other companies, regularly advertised in directories and guide books, in the days when the latter contained large sections of hotel, railway and shipping advertisements. In the last twenty or thirty years of the nineteenth century the publication of immensely detailed guide books such as Black's, Baedeker's and Murray's, was at its zenith, and they were widely used by the serious-minded tourist. By the first war their number had declined and in the more 'popular' type of guide book of later years there was no place for the advertisements which were such a feature of the Victorian guides.

The press advertisements were supplemented by printed handbills, and, for the more important announcements, letterpress posters, which were displayed on the bill boards on and around stations. Considering their ephemeral and fragile nature it is surprising that handbills still survive from the 1870s and 80s at least in sufficient numbers to give us a general idea of their typography and layout. They were printed mainly on strongly tinted papers, dark blues and greens, bright yellow, pink and buff being the most common. Excursion handbills had the destination in a very large condensed type, often printed from wood letter, and for the main body of the text the slab-serif or Egyptian types were very popular, with occasional lines in grotesque (sans serif) faces. There was no uniformity in design of the company's bills, even the words GREAT WESTERN RAILWAY being set in a variety of types according to the whim of the compositor. Even as late as 1914 the *Railway News*, in its jubilee issue, condemned railway handbills in which the details were 'displayed in such a conglomeration of type as to repel the most eager of potential passengers'.

Closely allied to the handbill were the excursion programmes. In the 1870s these were printed on tinted paper in the same format as the penny time book, with which they were bound as a supplement as well as being issued separately, but they were later reduced to the same size as handbills and their contents developed along the same lines. Although for a time in the 90s some descriptive matter was included in the programme, after the turn of the century this function was taken over by the illustrated folders and travel books, and the excursion programmes were concerned solely with fares and timetables. Some of the programmes of the 90s bore quite attractive covers with floral borders and a reasonably restrained use of type, but some were not in such good taste—an issue for July 1897 showed what the Victorian compositor could do when he chose to show off; the cover had no less than twenty assorted type-faces.

The larger bills, or posters, followed the same general design as handbills, with the addition of a word or two in one or even two contrasting colours. From the 1880s some time bills and other posters had elaborate two-colour ornamental headings printed from wood blocks. The layout and type-faces used in letterpress posters underwent surprisingly little change between the 1880s and the first war. Some of the Great Western bills were printed by large London firms, notably Waterlow, Wyman, McCorquodale and Judd & Co, but many came from provincial printers where wood letter tended to remain in use for very long periods.

A report of the advertising department for the half-year ending 31 January 1876 gives some interesting figures for that time. For each excursion train from London 700 posters and 18,500 handbills were printed, the posters costing £4 10s 0d (£4.50). This compared with 1,200 posters and 30,000 handbills distributed by the London & North Western for similar trains. At that time there were about 110 excursions from London in the half-year August-January. The same report gives the total expenditure on advertising in newspapers and guide books as £2,493. It also mentions that the advertising on the Bristol & Exeter, South Devon and Cornwall Railways was then being placed under Paddington control.

The stationery superintendent, W. H. Jarvis, writing in the *Magazine* in 1931, said that even by the end of the first war 'the printed announcements with which our stations were still too liberally bespattered were a blot on the edifice', and that something had to be done to bring order and uniformity to the company's bill boards and hoardings. This was a matter in which the new general manager, Felix Pole, took a personal interest, and it was at his suggestion that action was taken. It came none too soon, for the grouping was soon to bring many fresh ideas and new techniques into railway publicity, and Pole doubtless realised that the Great Western must refurbish its own advertising if it was to compete successfully with the new companies.

In October 1922 a new standard letterpress poster was designed, using a type known as Winchester Bold, and a reverse block (white letters on a coloured ground) for the company's name. Specimen designs were prepared for twelve types of bill, and these were circulated through divisions to the regular printers. These were the provincial firms who printed handbills, posters and the extra train notices, after which the contracts were usually known. Some of these firms worked for the GWR for very long periods, notably Chance & Bland of Gloucester, Martin Billing of Birmingham, Joseph Wones of West Bromwich and J. W. Arrowsmith of Bristol. This latter firm had printed for the company at least as early as 1854.

The new posters broke with the old tradition of using a number of different type-faces for emphasis and variety. Now this was achieved in a much simpler and more pleasing way by the use of the same face in varying sizes. To avoid undue monotony the bills were printed in different colours, but generally only one colour was used for each bill.

Up to this time the types used in all Great Western publicity had been many and varied, but in 1923 the company adopted Cheltenham as its standard general-purpose face. This type originated in America and was first cast in this country shortly after 1900. Although nowadays Cheltenham is frowned upon by typographers, it had a great vogue in pre-1939 publicity printing and was a useful jobbing face, especially in the bold version which was extensively used by the Great Western from 1923 until 1947. It was very similar to the Winchester type used for letterpress posters.

The idea of a standard type-face for publicity and general use was pioneered by the London Underground Railways, who employed the eminent calligrapher Edward Johnston to design a sans-serif alphabet which was used for station signs as well as printed matter, and is still much in evidence today. Ten years after the GWR had adopted Cheltenham the London & North Eastern chose Eric Gill's celebrated sans-serif letter for use in its publicity and general printing. Although the Great Western gradually introduced Gill Sans in the 1930s it never completely superseded Cheltenham and Winchester Bold.

Nowhere was the adoption of a standard type-face more effective than in the printing of handbills, which the public soon came to recognise by their house style even before they read the headline, and when the roundel monogram was added in 1933, Great Western handbills assumed their final, and most pleasing and legible form.

In 1933 the efficacy of posters was being increased by the erection of company bill boards away from stations, so as to bring Great Western services before members of the public who did not normally use the stations, and the GWR also rented advertising space in London tube trains and on buses and trams. Indeed, as the company approached its hundredth year, Great Western publicity in the orthodox fields of press and posters was at last catching up with its more unusual activities in book publishing.

A type of poster which has not yet been mentioned is the hand-written bill. These were produced under divisional arrangements to advertise special trains or particular travel bargains, and although only done in small quantities they had the advantage of being available at short notice. Extra large bills or streamers were also done in this way for special boards displayed in prominent positions at the larger stations.

The criticism often levelled at the railways that they used too many posters (they were the largest single users of this form of publicity) and not enough newspaper space, could partly be justi-fied on the grounds of cost. Letterpress bills were cheap and cost next to nothing to display on the companies' own premises or on road cartage vehicles, while at the same time they relieved the drabness of stations and gave passengers something to read while waiting for trains. The principal drawback was that the railways were to some extent preaching to the converted, since the majority of posters were on stations, and only people accustomed to travel-ling by rail generally saw them. This was increasingly true as the motor car drew more and more people away from the railways. There was also the tendency that when too many bills were dis-played on a single site the effect of any one poster tended to be diminished by the sea of print which confronted the passer-by.

The display of posters on stations was the responsibility of station masters, and although the majority took this task seriously and placed the bills in good positions, there was a small minority who took little interest in publicity so that much of the matter sent to them was wasted. As G. E. Orton pointed out in a lecture on publicity in 1934, the station master 'should realise that he is the local publicity officer'. This was true in more than one sense. Not only was the effective use of posters and other publicity matter largely dependent on station masters, but the cleanliness, tidiness and general efficiency of stations were themselves a vital part of railway publicity.

GREAT WESTERN RAILWAY.

ILFRACOMBE,
LYNTON
and
LYNMOUTH,

Per GREAT WESTERN RAILWAY to Portishead, *via* Bristol, and thence per commodious Steamship.

DAILY SERVICE
(Sundays excepted).

THROUGH FARES including Railways, Steamers, and all charges on Landing and Embarkation.

LONDON, Paddington, Westbourne Park, and Kensington. [Return and Circular Tickets at London Fares are also issued at Victoria, Uxbridge Rd., Moorgate St., Cook's Office, Ludgate Circus, Farringdon Street, Mansion House, Blackfriars, Charing Cross, Westminster Bridge.]	SINGLE.			RETURN. Available for Two Months.			CIRCULAR. Forward *via* Portishead, and return by Coach, and Devon and Somerset Railway or *vice versa*.	
	1st Class Best Cabin and Promenade Deck.	2nd Class Best Cabin and Promenade Deck.	3rd Class Fore Cabin and Main Deck.	1st Class Best Cabin and Promenade Deck.	2nd Class Best Cabin and Promenade Deck.	3rd Class Fore Cabin and Main Deck	1st Class	2nd Class
	S. D.	S. D.	S. D.	S. D.	S. D.	S. D.	S. D.	S. D.
	29 6	24 6	15 0	43 6	36 0	22 6	49 3	38 0
OXFORD	24 0	20 6	13 0	35 6	29 9	19 6	45 0	36 6
READING	25 6	21 6	13 6	37 6	31 9	20 3	46 0	36 6
WARWICK	32 0	26 0	16 0	47 6	38 3	24 0	54 6	43 0
LEAMINGTON	32 0	26 0	16 0	47 6	38 3	24 0	54 6	43 0
BANBURY	28 6	23 6	14 6	42 6	34 9	22 6	52 0	41 6
STROUD	20 0	17 0	11 0	29 6	24 9	16 0	36 0	30 0
CIRENCESTER	19 6	16 6	10 6	28 0	24 3	15 9	36 6	30 6
SWINDON	18 6	16 0	10 0	27 0	23 3	15 3	35 6	29 6
CHIPPENHAM	15 6	13 6	8 6	23 0	19 6	13 3	31 0	25 6
BATH	11 6	10 6	7 6	17 6	15 6	10 6	26 6	22 6
NEWPORT	15 0	12 6	9 0	22 0	18 6	13 0	28 9	24 3
CHEPSTOW	13 6	12 0	8 6	19 6	17 6	12 6	23 6	19 6
CHEDDAR	...	...	...	19 0	17 0	12 9	23 6	19 6
CLEVEDON	...	...	...	17 6	16 0	11 9	22 0	18 6
HIGHBRIDGE	...	...	...	22 3	19 3	13 6	22 0	18 6
WELLS (B. & E.)	...	...	...	21 0	18 3	14 0	26 6	22 0
WESTON-SUPER-MARE	...	...	...	19 0	17 0	12 3	22 0	18 6
BRIDGEWATER	...	...	...	25 3	22 6	15 0	22 0	18 6

The Steamer will start from Portishead Pier about 1.15 p.m., after the arrival of the Trains leaving Paddington at 9.0 a.m.; Oxford, 9.30; Reading, 9.50; Warwick, 7.36; Leamington, 8.0; Banbury, 8.29; Stroud, 8.7; Cirencester, 7.50; Swindon, 10.55; Chippenham, 9.45; Bath, 11.35; Wells (B. & E.), 9.55; Highbridge, 10.42; Weston-Super-Mare, 10.45; Cheddar, 10.23; Clevedon, 11.0; and Bridgwater at 10.29 a.m.

PADDINGTON, *July*, 1878.

J. GRIERSON, *General Manager.*

Waterlow and Sons Limited, Printers, London Wall, London.

Small bill, 1878. Printed by Waterlow, black on yellow

Page 53 (above) *Three early pictorial folders, c 1912;* (below) *folders for Cornish Riviera (1926) South Wales (1939) and containers (1939)*

Page 54 (above left) *Camping coach booklet, 1934;* (right) *Coronation tours booklet, 1937;* (below left) *illustrated booklet for the visit of* King George V *to America, 1927;* (below right) *camping holidays booklet, 1934*

GREAT WESTERN RAILWAY.

SUMMER EXCURSIONS

TO

TINTERN

Via THE WYE VALLEY RAILWAY,

AT REDUCED FARES,

From JUNE 4th until further Notice.

From Bristol, Lawrence Hill, Stapleton Road, Clifton Down, and Montpelier	On Mondays and Saturdays.
„ Bath	On Tuesdays and Wednesdays.
„ Cheltenham, Cirencester & Stroud	On Tuesdays.
„ Newport and Gloucester... ...	On Thursdays.
„ Cardiff	On Wednesdays.
„ Hereford	On Mondays and Thursdays.
„ Ross	

TIMES AND FARES.

	First Class.		Second Class.		Third Class.		Return Train from Tintern.
	a.m. a.m.	s.	d.	s.	d.	s.	d.	
From Bristol 7 15 9 45							4 27 or 7 35 p.m.
„ Lawrence Hill 7 20 9 50							4 27 or 7 35 p.m.
„ Stapleton Road 7 25 9 55	5	0	3	6	2	6	4 27 or 7 35 p.m.
„ Clifton Down... 7 0 9 30							4 27 p.m.
„ Montpelier ... 7 3 9 33							4 27 p.m.
„ Bath 6 35 8 35	6	0	4	6	3	0	4 27 or 7 35 p.m.
„ Cheltenham ... 8 45	7	0	5	0	3	6	4 27 or 7 35 p.m.
	p.m.							
„ Newport 10 40 1 25	5	0	3	6	2	6	4 27 or 7 35 p.m.
„ Cardiff 10 15 12 50	6	0	4	6	3	0	4 27 or 7 35 p.m.
	a.m.							
„ Hereford 6 20 11 0	6	0	4	6	3	0	5 50 p.m.
„ Ross 8 35 11 45	5	0	3	6	2	6	5 50 p.m.
„ Gloucester...... 9 15	6	0	4	6	3	0	4 27 or 7 35 p.m.
„ Cirencester ... 7 50	8	0	6	0	4	0	4 27 p.m.
„ Stroud 8 40	7	0	5	0	3	6	4 27 or 7 35 p.m.

Clifton Down and Montpelier Passengers change into the South Wales Union Trains at Stapleton Road. The last Return Train by which there is any connection to Clifton Down or Montpelier leaves Tintern at 4.27 p.m., but Passengers may, if they like, return to Stapleton Road by the Train leaving Tintern at 7.35 p.m.

NOTE.—The 7.15 a.m. Train from Bristol does not run beyond Chepstow, but Passengers are booked through to Tintern by that Train to enable them to visit Chepstow, and they can proceed to Tintern by the 11.22 a.m. Train from Chepstow.

The Tickets are only available on the day of issue, and by the specified Trains, and are not transferable. **Passengers passing through Chepstow may stop there either going or returning.**

J. GRIERSON,

PADDINGTON, *May*, 1879.   GENERAL MANAGER.

Waterlow & Sons Limited, Printers, London Wall, London.

Handbill, 1879. Printed by Waterlow, black on yellow

D

T. 5491
70

GREAT WESTERN RAILWAY.

FLOWER SHOW

At NEWPORT.

On THURSDAY, JULY 17th, 1884,

RETURN TICKETS

At a Single Fare and a Quarter

(1st, 2nd, and 3rd Class)

WILL BE ISSUED TO

NEWPORT

From the undermentioned Stations—

STATIONS.	By Train leaving at	Times of Return Trains.
	a.m. p.m.	p.m. p.m.
EBBW VALE	11 17 and 1 27	
VICTORIA	11 24 and 1 34	p.m. p.m.
CWM	11 29 and 1 39	
NANTYGLO	11 17 and 1 27	6 5 and 8 5
BLAINA	11 23 and 1 33	
ABERTILLERY	11 32 and 1 42	
ABERBEEG	11 42 and 1 52	
BLAENAVON	11 30	
CWMAVON	11 39	
ABERSYCHAN	11 45	6 5 and 8 45
PONTNEWYNYDD	11 50	
PONTYPOOL (Crane Street) ...	11 57 and 2 58	
	p.m.	
ABERGAVENNY	12 8 and 1 33	
PEMPERGWM	12 15	5 27 and 7 10
NANTYDERRY	12 23	
PONTYPOOL ROAD ...	12 33	
CARDIFF	12 15 and 2 45	6 52 and 7 50
CHEPSTOW	12 16	6 33
PORTSKEWETT	12 40	7 5 and 8 3

Tickets are not transferable, and are only available to and from the Stations named upon them, by the above Trains and on the day of issue; if otherwise used the full Ordinary Fares will be charged.

PADDINGTON, *July*, 1884.

J. GRIERSON, General Manager

Waterlow and Sons Limited, Printers, London Wall, London.

Small bill, 1884. Printed by Waterlow, black on cream

GREAT WESTERN RAILWAY.

HEREFORD REGATTA.

ON THURSDAY, JULY 28TH, 1892,

RETURN TICKETS

WILL BE ISSUED TO

HEREFORD

At about a Single Fare and a Quarter for the Double Journey.

AS UNDER:—

FROM				TIMES.	
				A.M.	A.M.
PRESTEIGN	.	.	.	7 25	11 0
KINGTON	.	.	.	7 55	11 15
TITLEY	.	.	.	8 0	11 20
PEMBRIDGE	.	.	.	8 9	11 31
KINGSLAND	.	.	.	8 16	11 40
BARBERS BRIDGE	.	.	.	7 36	10 49
NEWENT	.	.	.	7 47	10 58
DYMOCK	.	.	.	7 55	11 7
WORCESTER (Shrub Hill)		.	.	7 33	9 50
,, (Foregate St.)		.	.	7 36	9 53
HENWICK	.	.	.	7 41	9 58
MALVERN LINK	.	.	.	7 59	10 10
GREAT MALVERN	.	.	.	8 8	10 17
MALVERN WELLS	,	.	.	8 12	10 21
COLWALL	.	.	.	8 18	10 26
LEDBURY	.	.	.	8 30	10 36
ASHPERTON	.	.	.	8 38	10 44
STOKE EDITH	.	.	.	8 44	10 50

The Tickets are available for Return on the day of issue only by any Ordinary Train (as per Time Bills) with a connection to the Stations named.

The Tickets are not Transferable, and are available only by the Trains specified, and between the Stations named upon them; if used otherwise, the full Ordinary Fare will be charged.

Children under Three years of age, Free; Three and under Twelve, Half-price.

PADDINGTON,
July, 1892.

Hy. LAMBERT, General Manager.

(H.D. 128)   JUDD & Co., Limited, Printers, 63, Carter Lane, Doctors' Commons, E.C.   [919a.]

Small bill, 1892. Printed by Judd & Co, black on dull green. Note the use of an outmoded fat-face type for HEREFORD

~*~ G. W. R. ~*~

Excursion to the South Coast.

On SATURDAY, July 25,

A DAY-TRIP EXCURSION will run to

BOURNEMOUTH

(WEST)

BY THE DIRECT ROUTE VIA SALISBURY.

LEAVING	AT	Return Fare, 3rd Class.
	A.M.	
Cheddar	5 52	
Axbridge	6 0	
Winscombe	6 8	**4/3**
Sandford and Banwell ..	6 12	
Congresbury	6 20	
Yatton	6 25	

The Return Train will leave Bournemouth (West) at 8.55 p.m. the same day.

Children under Twelve Years of age, Half-price.

No Luggage Allowed.

The Tickets are not transferable. Should an Excursion or Cheap Ticket be used for any other Station than those named upon it, or by any other Train than those specified, it will be rendered void, and therefore the fare paid will be liable to forfeiture, and the full Ordinary Fare will become chargeable.

The issuing of Through Tickets is subject to the conditions and regulations set out in the Time Tables Books, Bills, and Notices of the respective Companies and Proprietors on whose Railways, Coaches, or Steam boats they are available, and the holder, by accepting a Through Ticket, agrees that the respective Companies and Proprietors are not to be held liable for any loss, damage, injury, delay, or detention, caused or arising off their respective Railways, Coaches, or Steamboats. The contract and liability of each Company and Proprietor are limited to their or his own Railways, Coaches, or Steamboats.

For any further information respecting the arrangements shewn in this bill, application should be made at any of the Company's offices or agencies, to Mr. C. KISLINGBURY, Divisional Superintendent, G.W.R. Temple Meads Station, Bristol, or to Mr. J. MORRIS, Superintendent of the Line, Paddington Station, W.

Paddington, July, 1908.   JAMES C. INGLIS, General Manager.
(Bristol—1,000 R. 8vo, 2 pp.)   Arrowsmith, Printer, Quay Street, Bristol.   (B 531)

Side panel:

NOW Ready

1908 Edition

HOLIDAY **H**AUNTS

IN

ENGLAND, WALES, IRELAND, BRITTANY

Nearly **600** *pages.*

Contains list of RESORTS, HOTELS, LODGINGS, GOLF LINKS, Etc.

PRICE 3d.

at principal Stations and Offices.

Handbill, 1908. Printed by Arrowsmith, Bristol, black on orange. Note the panel containing publicity for *Holiday Haunts*. A map of the Fishguard route to Ireland appeared on the reverse

Great Western Railway

TRAIN SERVICE BETWEEN

ABERYSTWYTH

—— AND ——

DEVIL'S BRIDGE

July 8th to September 21st, inclusive.

		Week-days.								Sundays.
		B a.m.	G a.m.	S a.m.	G a.m.	G p.m.	p.m.	G p.m.	p.m.	A p.m.
ABERYSTWYTH	dep.	7 20	10⁻ 0	10 0	10 20	2 0	2 30	5 5	6 10	2 30
Llanbadarn	,,	7 27	—	10 7	10 27	—	2 37	5 12	6 17	2 37
Glanrafon	,,	7 32	—	10 12	10 32	—	2 42	5 17	6 22	—
Capel Bangor	,,	7 40	—	10 20	10 40	—	2 50	5 25	6 30	2 50
Nantyronen	,,	7 49	—	10 29	10 49	—	2 59	—	6 39	—
Aberffrwd	,,	7 54	—.	10 34	10 54	—	3 4	5 42	6 44	3 5
Rheidol Falls	,,	8 10	—	10 50	11 10	—	3 20	—	7 0	3 20
Rhiwfron	,,	8 21	—	11 1	11 21	—	3 31	—	7 11	—
DEVIL'S BRIDGE	arr.	8 25	11 0	11 5	11 25	3 0	3 35	6 11	7 15	3 35

A—Sundays, July 21st to Sept. 1st, inclusive.

		B a.m.	a.m.	G p.m.	G p.m.	p.m.	G p.m.	p.m.	A p.m.
DEVIL'S BRIDGE	dep.	8 40	11 30	12 30	3 40	4 45	6 20	7 35	5 30
Rhiwfron	,,	8 44	11 34	12 34	3 44	4 49	6 24	7 39	—
Rheidol Falls	,,	8 55	11 34	12 45	3 55	5 0	6 35	7 50	5 44
Aberffrwd	,,	9 5	11 55	12 55	4 5	5 10	6 45	8 0	5 54
Nantyronen	,,	9 14	12 4	1 4	4 14	5 19	6 54	8 9	—
Capel Bangor	,,	9 22	12 12	1 12	4 22	5 27	7 2	8 17	6 11
Glanrafon	,,	9 31	12 21	1 21	4 31	5 36	7 11	8 26	—
Llanbadarn	,,	9 36	12 26	1 26	4 36	5 41	7 16	8 31	6 25
ABERYSTWYTH	arr.	9 42	12 32	1 32	4 42	5 47	7 22	8 37	6 30

A—Sundays, July 21st to Sept. 1st, inclusive.

B—Mondays only.   G—Saturdays excepted.   S—Saturdays only.

Cheap Day Return Fare
2/6—Third Class
Aberystwyth and Devil's Bridge.

Combined Rail and Scenery Ticket

ISSUED ON FRIDAYS AND SATURDAYS, JULY 12th TO SEPTEMBER 21st, AND ON
SUNDAYS, JULY 21st TO SEPTEMBER 1st

TRAINS AS SHOWN ABOVE.   INCLUSIVE FARE 3/-

This Ticket enables the visitor to view the famous Devil's Bridge Waterfalls and Scenery.

For any further information respecting the arrangements shewn in this Bill, application should be made at any
of the Company's Stations or Offices ; to
Mr. H. WARWICK, District Traffic Manager, G.W.R., Oswestry ; or to
Mr. R. H. NICHOLLS, Superintendent of the Line, Paddington Station, W.

Paddington Station, June, 1929.   FELIX J. C. POLE, General Manager.

No. 198 (5,000) Oswestry 25/6/29.   Printed by Joseph Wones, West Bromwich also at Birmingham and London.

Handbill, 1929. Printed by Joseph Wones, West Bromwich, blue on white. A
somewhat uninteresting bill from the period preceding the introduction of the
roundel

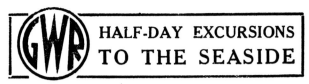

GWR HALF-DAY EXCURSIONS TO THE SEASIDE

SUNDAY, JULY 14th

To BRISTOL, WESTON-super-MARE

AND

BURNHAM-ON-SEA

ENJOY OCEAN BREEZES AT THE OLD PIER, WESTON-SUPER-MARE.
THE SEA IS ALWAYS IN.   TRIPS BY STEAMERS, SPEED BOATS, ETC.

FROM	AT	RETURN FARES—Third Class.			Return Train due to arrive at
		Bristol (Stapleton Rd.)	Weston-s-Mare (General)	Burnham-on-Sea	
	a.m.	s. d.	s. d.	s. d.	p.m.
STONEHOUSE	9 45	3 6	4 0	4 6	10 23
STROUD	9 55	3 6	4 0	4 6	10 16
BRIMSCOMBE	10 0	3 6	4 0	4 6	10 10
CHALFORD	10 5	3 6	4 0	4 6	10 7
CIRENCESTER TOWN ..	10* 0	4 0	4 6	4 6	10* 5
KEMBLE	10 20	3 6	4 0	4 6	9 50
OAKSEY HALT	10 25	3 6	4 0	4 6	9 45
MINETY AND ASHTON KEYNES	10 30	3 6	4 0	4 6	9 30
PURTON	10 40	3 6	4 0	4 6	9 20
Arrival Times	..	11.52 a.m.	12.37 p.m.	1.10 p.m.	
Return Times same day	..	8.10 p.m.	7.25 p.m.	6.55 p.m.	

*—Change at Kemble in each direction.

IN CONNECTION WITH THIS TRIP

COMBINED RAIL AND ROAD BOOKINGS WILL BE GIVEN TO CHEDDAR AND TO WELLS, VIA WESTON-SUPER-MARE.

Inclusive Tickets will be issued at all the stations mentioned above, and the combined fares will be the advertised Excursion fare to Weston-super-Mare, plus the proportions shewn below :—

WESTON-SUPER-MARE TO CHEDDAR AND BACK 1/9	Children under 14 years of age Half-fare.	WESTON-SUPER-MARE TO WELLS AND BACK 2/9

Passengers make their own way between Weston-super-Mare Station and the Beach 'Bus Station (about ten minutes' walk) and travel by any of advertised Omnibus Services of the Bristol Tramway & Carriage Company to and from Cheddar or Wells (according to ticket held).

Times of suitable services are shewn hereunder :—

		p.m.	p.m.	p.m.	p.m.	
Weston-s.-Mare (Beach Station)	dep.	1 30	2 0	3 0	3 30	..
Cheddar (Cliff Street)	arr.	2 23	2 51	3 51	4 23	..
Wells (Square)	arr.	..	3 22	4 22	..	..

		p.m.	p.m.	p.m.	p.m.	
Wells (Square)	dep.	3 30	..	4 30	5 30	..
Cheddar (Cliff Street)	dep.	4 1	4 30	5 1	6 1	..
Weston-s.-Mare (Beach Station)	arr.	4 53	5 23	5 53	6 53	..

Any further information may be obtained from **Mr. H. Williams**, Divisional Superintendent, Northgate Mansions, Gloucester (Telephone 3056, Extension 30B) ; or from **Mr. H. L. Wilkinson**, Superintendent of the Line, Paddington Station, W.2.

NOTICE AS TO CONDITIONS.—Children under 3 years of age, Free ; Three and under 14 years of age, Half-price. Tickets are not transferable. These tickets are issued at less than the ordinary fares, and are subject to the Notices and Conditions shewn in the current Time Tables. No luggage allowed except small handbags, luncheon baskets or other small articles intended for the passenger's personal use during the day. On the RETURN journey passengers may take with them, free of charge, at Owner's Risk, goods not exceeding in the aggregate 60 lbs. which they may have purchased for their own use (not for sale).

Paddington Station, W.2., July, 1935.   JAMES MILNE, General Manager.

G. 12/286. G.D. 2,500.   Printed by Chance & Bland (Printers) Ltd., Gloucester.

Handbill, 1935. Printed by Chance & Bland, Gloucester, crimson on white. The final form of Great Western handbill introduced in 1933

Standard Tourist Programme covers: *right* as used in late 1920s and early 30s; *left* simpler layout set throughout in Cheltenham Bold type and incorporating the roundel

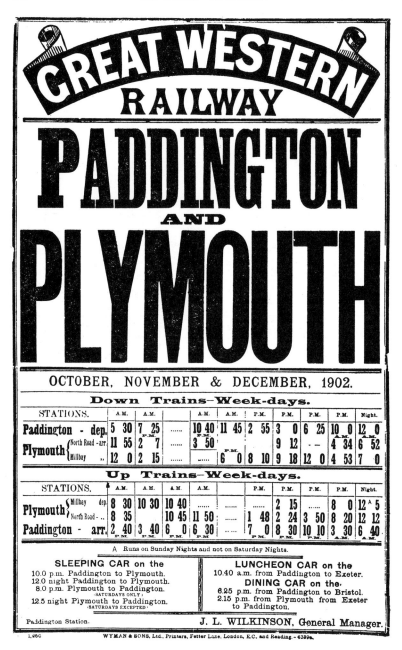

Letterpress poster, 1902. Printed by Wyman, heading and PLYMOUTH in scarlet, remainder in green, on white paper

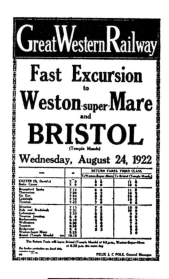

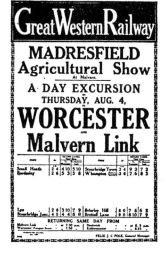

Standard letterpress bills set in Winchester type introduced in 1922 (GWR *Magazine*)

THURSDAY

SEPTEMBER 7th

Restaurant Car

HALF-DAY

EXCURSION

TO

BRISTOL

LEAVING AT	FROM	RETURN FARES Third Class		RETURN TRAINS	
				BRISTOL (T.M.) dep. 7-10 p.m.	BRISTOL (T.M.) dep. 9§0 p.m.
a.m.		s.	d.	arrive p.m.	arrive night
10 35	PLYMOUTH (North Road)	7	3	10* 25	12† 29
11 10	TOTNES - - -	6	3	9 45	11 50

BRISTOL (Temple Meads) arrive 2-0 p.m.; return 7-10 or 9§0 p.m.

*—Millbay arrive 10-32 p.m.   †—Millbay arrive 12-40 night.   §—No Restaurant Car on this service.

"IT'S QUICKER BY RAIL"

FOR FURTHER PARTICULARS, SEE HANDBILLS OBTAINABLE AT STATIONS AND OFFICES

PADDINGTON STATION
August 1939   335—60   JAMES MILNE, General Manager.

Printed in Great Britain by Latimer, Trend & Co., Ltd., Plymouth.

Typical standard poster of the final style. Printed by Latimer Trend, Plymouth, in scarlet on white paper. This excursion presumably never ran, as war was declared four days before

Chapter 3

Pictorial Posters, Folders and Booklets

PICTORIAL POSTERS

Of the many forms of publicity used by the railway companies it is probably the pictorial poster which is most readily called to mind by the general public. This is not to say, however, that posters were the form of advertising which gave the best returns in terms of additional traffic. Indeed, the relative merits of posters, press advertisements and other forms of publicity were debated vigorously in railway and advertising circles for many years. It is a pity that comparatively few of the posters, particularly those of early date, have survived.

Pictorial posters were the creation of the last quarter of the nineteenth century, and were a direct result of the perfection of colour lithography. Early development took place in France under the influence of Jules Chéret and later of Toulouse-Lautrec and others. In Britain pictorial theatre and other bills began to enliven the streets in the 1890s, with John Hassall, Cecil Aldin and the Beggarstaffs (William Nicholson and James Pryde) among the leading exponents in the new medium. Commercial concerns took up the idea and the use of pictorial posters soon spread rapidly. It also became the fashion to collect posters, just as people were collecting picture post-cards at that time.

In the pre-grouping days the railways did make use of the pictorial poster, generally with no great distinction, though there was the occasional masterpiece like John Hassall's famous 'Skegness is *so* Bracing' done for the Great Northern Railway in 1908, which retained its appeal well into LNER days. Hassall, with his humorous approach and his technique of employing flat colour

65

and clean line, established himself as a master in this field.

Exactly when the Great Western issued its first pictorial poster is uncertain. A statement in the *Magazine* in May 1907 that 'The Great Western Railway have been pioneers in poster improvement from the very first' is tantalisingly vague. The Ascot Races bill dated June 1897, preserved in the GWR Museum at Swindon is said to be the earliest surviving example, and there is a record of coloured posters for Cornwall, the Channel Islands and Wales of about the same date. But there had been occasional letterpress bills incorporating a coloured lithograph well before this, a surviving example being a poster for the Royal Tournament dated June 1889 which has as a central vignette a coloured lithograph of a scene from that event.

The Ascot bill was a superb example of the art of the lithographer, but it was excessively ornate and hardly the kind of poster to be read at a glance. Fortunately the *Magazine* issued two supplements, in 1907-8, each reproducing six Great Western posters in full colour, and they illustrate this tendency very clearly. Small though they are, these reproductions are probably the only evidence we now have for judging the company's earliest efforts in pictorial advertising. (see page 18)

These early posters all suffered from excessive detail, and lettering which was ill-fitted to its purpose (it would have been more suitable for titling a Walt Disney cartoon than for a railway poster). The lettering being superimposed on the picture only added to the confusion. Yet such was the taste of the day that a writer in the *Magazine*, while admitting that the lettering was 'somewhat difficult to make out', dismissed this as 'of small importance'. It is also significant that none of the dozen reproduced in the *Magazine* showed any railway stock or equipment, except one bill for the Llandyssul to New Quay road motor service, in which one of the three separate pictures depicted a motor bus. Another serious fault was the use of these composite designs, with several separate scenes on one poster.

The designer of the six 1908 bills is not stated, but the 1907 batch were all by Alec Fraser, and lithographed by Andrew Reid & Co Ltd of Newcastle-upon-Tyne. That the company was pleased with them is indicated by the fact that the original paintings were displayed in the booking hall at Paddington. Alec Fraser was responsible for most of the first generation of Great Western posters, and many of these were printed by Andrew Reid, whose advertisement, incidentally, can be seen in the GWR *Magazine* over a long period. The subjects were, of course, the Great Western's usual ones—Devon and Cornwall, North Wales, the Upper Thames, Southern Ireland and Brittany. Some originality was shown in a quad royal poster for Brittany, in which the similarity of St Michael's Mount and Mont St Michel were put to good use, as was the striking resemblance (though in reverse) of the shape of Cornwall and Italy. The statement that there was a similar likeness in climate and natural beauty was, perhaps, a little far-fetched. The number of posters distributed at that time can be judged from the printing order for the Brittany bill: in 1908 5,000 quad royal and 3,000 8-sheet were printed at a cost of £100 and £105 respectively, and a further 3,000 8-sheet were produced in 1910 at a cost of £115.

The remaining years before the first war produced little general improvement, though the occasional poster stood out from the rest. In 1911 a particularly charming design to advertise the Plymouth—Brest steamer service was issued, with a painting by Dorothee George of two Breton girls in national costume. It was uncluttered by lettering, which was confined to panels at the top and bottom. There was also a poster by Alec Fraser for the Fishguard—Rosslare service, showing the terminal station, the Fishguard Bay Hotel and a Great Western steamer setting out across the harbour with the *Mauretania* beyond the breakwater.

Posters issued jointly with municipalities made their appearance at this period. One such, issued in 1908, was for Wolverhampton. It showed three separate scenes in the town, with the caption 'Excellent Corridor Train Service by G.W.R.' A series of hotel posters, presumably issued for mutual benefit, appeared in 1909, including one for the Grand Hotel, Birmingham, which was close to Snow Hill station. At that time much effort was going into publicising the two-hour expresses to Birmingham, and a quad royal poster was produced in 1910 carrying a route map of the Bicester line and an excess of lettering which marred a promising idea.

The press evidently kept an eye open for particularly striking posters, and comment was especially favourable on an Easter Holidays bill issued in 1911, using, for a change, bold script lettering, a spray of Easter lilies and a vignette of the 'Riviera' at speed. April of that year was exceptionally cold, and the issue at short notice of a simple circular bill headed 'The Arctic April' and saying in a few words that it was warm and sunny in the Cornish Riviera, prompted the *Railway Gazette* to call it 'smart publicity work by the G.W.R.' Naturally, the Great Western did not have it all their own way, and even Cornwall's mild climate had its rival; the LNWR made equally strong claims for North Wales as a winter resort, and published a well-illustrated book on the area.

By this time *Holiday Haunts*, first published in 1906, had become sufficiently important to justify a poster to increase its sales, and the 1911 edition was advertised by a bill reproducing the cover against a seashore background.

Pictorial posters suffered the same eclipse during the first war as did other forms of publicity, but it could be said that the long break had a beneficial effect, for the immediate post-war productions bore little resemblance to the designs of the pre-1914 era. Gone were the fussy detail and the excessive and sometimes illegible lettering. Poster designers had turned to a simpler, bolder approach clearly derived from the demands of wartime propaganda posters.

The first few years after the end of the war were full of change, and of challenge. There were two changes in general manager: Frank Potter was succeeded by Charles Aldington in August 1919, and Felix Pole took office after Aldington's resignation owing to ill-health in June 1921. In August of that year the Railways Act became law, to be followed only eighteen months later by the grouping. 1924 saw the enlargement of the old GWR advertising department into the new publicity department and the appointment of W. H. Fraser as publicity agent. In many respects the company's publicity made significant strides, but improvement in poster design was slow, spasmodic and without any apparent policy.

Felix Pole's concern to improve Great Western publicity is

indicated by his sponsoring of a competition for poster designs, with a first prize of no less than a hundred guineas, which was announced in the *Magazine* in April 1922. Over 3,000 entries were received, but none of the designs was ever used. Certainly this procedure was not calculated to ensure the regular supply of good posters to match those coming from the newly-created group companies, who were using much more professional methods.

There is no doubt that had the war not intervened, the company would very soon have found itself sadly behind current trends. In 1913 Frank Pick, who joined the London Underground Railways in 1906 and later became managing director, began commissioning artists of the highest calibre to design posters for his group, and very quickly the Underground gained a clear lead in publicity over the other railway companies. Their posters, by such artists as Fred Taylor, Gregory Brown, and particularly E. McKnight Kauffer, set an entirely new standard which amounted to a renaissance in poster art. Little wonder that a contemporary writer described the Underground, with its hundred new posters a year, as 'London's most popular art gallery'.

The lead given by the Underground was matched after the grouping by entirely new concepts in railway advertising which were developed by the LNER and LMS. The posters issued by these companies reflected a much more professional approach to the subject than had ever been shown by the Great Western, or indeed any other company. In the case of the LNER, the progressive policy was largely due to their advertising manager, W. M. Teasdale, who very quickly put his new company well ahead with a series of first class posters designed by artists who were the acknowledged leaders of their profession. Fred Taylor's 'Scarborough', Frank Brangwyn's 'Royal Border Bridge' and Frank Newbould's 'Old Bridge on the Dee' were among the finest posters ever executed for a railway company, and were done within a year or two of the formation of the LNER. By employing these, and other comparable artists like Tom Purvis and Frank Mason, and by paying some of them retaining fees, the LNER was assured of a succession of fine posters throughout the inter-war years.

The LMS went about its poster production in a different, and original way. Norman Wilkinson RI was commissioned to select a number of Royal Academicians and ARAs to produce original paintings for the company. This novel idea was, needless to say, a great success, and it was responsible for some fine posters. The artists who worked for the LMS at this time included some very eminent names—Augustus John, Sir D. Y. Cameron, Sir William Orpen and Norman Wilkinson himself, whose 'Galloway' was a superbly simple and effective poster.

The improvements in poster art initiated by the LNER and LMS were not lost on the art critics of the day. Walter Shaw Sparrow opens the paragraph on railways in his *Advertising and British Art* (1924) with these telling words: 'As for our railways, the Great Western has not yet explored any of the great opportunities that its country-side and seasides offer. Its posters are less attractive by far than its pamphlets and guides . . . I am told that the Great Western Railway intends to improve greatly the whole of its advertising'. The last remark was no doubt an allusion to the reorganisation at Paddington and the appointment of Fraser. Perhaps the only crumb of comfort which the GWR could draw from this is that at least the author mentioned the Great Western first. The other group companies were only a year or so old in 1924, and their names were unfamiliar, but the fact remains that in this book, as in the several others on poster art published in the 1920s, LNER and LMS posters were reproduced frequently, and received warm and well-merited approval from the critics. The Great Western, alas, was conspicuous by its absence.

In spite of the standards set by their new rivals, it cannot be said that Paddington rose to the challenge with any degree of determination. There had always been a degree of amateurism in the company's publicity, and while this does not seem to have impeded progress in some other forms of publicity, it certainly had a disastrous effect on the company's posters. The publicity department lacked the artistic leadership so evident in the LNER under Teasdale, and much of the poster work was put out to printers who specialised in this work and had their own regular artists, not, regrettably, in the first class, who worked up designs from rough ideas submitted by the publicity department. This unsatisfactory arrangement finally ceased when the stationery

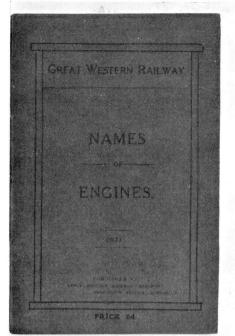

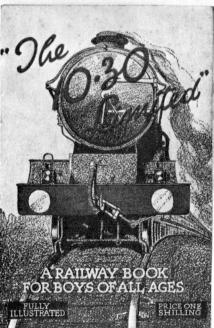

Page 71 (above) *First and last editions of the Engine Book, 1911 and 1946, the latter having a cover by Charles Mayo;* (below left) *W. G. Chapman's first book, 1923;* (right) *typical cover of the* Rambles *series, 1938*

THE CORNISH

RIVIERA

S.P.B.MAIS

DEVON

THE SHIRE OF THE SEA KINGS

Its Sunny Shores,
Bracing Moorlands and
Historic Sites.

(FIFTH EDITION.)

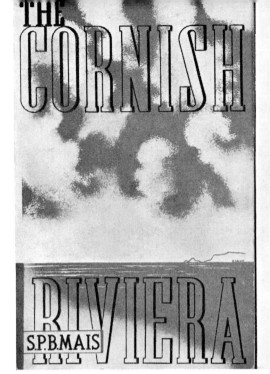

Page 72 (above left) *Cover by E. McKnight Kauffer for the third edition of* The Cornish Riviera, *1934; (right)* standard cover for A. M. Broadley's books; *(below)* gravure plate *and line drawings in the first edition of S. P. B. Mais'* The Cornish Riviera, *1928*

CHAPTER X

FROM ST. IVES TO NEWQUAY

ST. IVES has dignity, beauty, and a more than usually honourable history, and the fact that John Wesley visited it no less than twenty-seven times showed that he thought it worth converting. Like Newlyn, its industries are evenly divided between painting and fishing, but its fishing, to judge from the visitors, takes precedence. It is doubtful whether there is a more popular seaside resort in England. It is a place to which one gives one's love and loyalty at once, never to retract or forswear allegiance in spite of streets that are crowded almost to bursting-point in the height

of the season. It is easily the best centre for the extreme west of Cornwall, partly because of its own inherent loveliness, partly because the natives go so far out of their way to ensure their visitors' comfort. If ever there was a place where one feels instantly at home it is St. Ives.

It got its name

ST. IVES

102

The Coast at Clodgy, St. Ives

department took over responsibility for all the company's printing and put posters out to competitive tender.

It would be unfair to lay all the blame on the department. Publicity was not the highly developed profession it is today. Few people understood the potentialities of skilled and co-ordinated advertising, and fewer still knew how to put it into effect. On the Great Western there was a constant demand for economy which hampered Fraser and his successors, and there was a marked conservatism which resulted in any real departure from tradition being doomed to failure. Co-ordination between the different forms of advertising was lacking, with the result that it was not uncommon for a pictorial poster to be issued without supporting literature, and vice versa.

The later 1920s were therefore not very productive of good posters. When, however, the company did commission good artists the results were well up to the standard of the other companies but, no doubt for economic reasons, their posters were outnumbered by many far less satisfactory productions, including some particularly poor designs in which small half-tone reproductions of photographs were utilised. A glaring example of this was a bill issued in 1923 with the doubtful purpose of encouraging 'Bathing in February in the Cornish Riviera', in which no less than five bathing scenes were arranged like a page from a family album. The young ladies' bathing attire, no doubt in the latest fashion at the time, only adds to the quaintness of the design by present-day standards. (see page 35)

Fred Taylor, perhaps the leading poster artist of his time, was brought in to produce a number of posters, including a fine study of Exeter cathedral issued in 1926 (and later used for one of the first jig-saw puzzles), and posters for Bath and Warwick Castle. Among the other artists employed at this time was Graham Petrie, whose poster for Malvern (1925) showed what could be done in the field of holiday resort publicity.

A large proportion of pictorial posters was devoted to advertising the inland and seaside resorts, and a good deal of this was done in collaboration with the local authorities concerned, who shared the cost with the Great Western. Here again, financial considerations hampered the publicity department, as their designs

E

for the posters had to be approved by the appropriate town council, who were often opposed to anything which smacked of the *avant garde*. The authorities at Paddington, too, were deeply committed to the pursuit of realism in poster design, and this particular brand of Great Western conservatism made it very difficult for the department to employ such fine practitioners of poster art as E. McKnight Kauffer, the American artist, already mentioned in connection with the Underground, who had led the field for many years in progressive poster work. Although Kauffer did a series for the GWR, his designs had often to be watered down to suit Paddington tastes, and they met quite fierce criticism from both inside and outside the company. But the mere fact that his posters provoked comment showed that they were attracting attention, and that, after all, was their purpose.

By the 1930s the tide was turning, and the decade before the second world war brought to the Great Western's hoardings a good number of competent, and a few outstanding, posters. Among the most successful were designs by Frank Newbould, whose broad and colourful landscapes now enlivened Great Western stations as they had done those of the LNER a decade before.

Noteworthy among the other artists employed were Warwick Goble, who did a fine bill for Chepstow racecourse, P. Irwin Brown, who painted a series of four for the ever-popular Devon, Cornwall, Somerset and Wales, and Michael Reilly, who was to design many excellent posters for the GWR in the 1930s. Notable at this time also were J. P. Sayer's picture maps of Devon and Cornwall (1933) and Claude Buckle's 'Christ Church Quad, Oxford' and his poster for Bath (1932).

A superb quad royal poster of Saltash Bridge by Avan Anrooy, issued in 1931, was one of the first to incorporate the roundel monogram which was subsequently used on almost all new posters, and Frank Newbould did a fine bill for Cornwall which was to be followed by many more. For the centenary in 1935 M. Secretan, familiar to railway enthusiasts for his little sketches in the *Railway Magazine* and for his locomotive post-cards, designed a poster in which photography and painting were combined. It showed the 'Riviera', headed by *King Charles II*, emerging from Parson's tunnel between Dawlish and Teignmouth. In a panel below was a small drawing of the broad gauge *North Star*, the monogram and the words '100 Years of Progress, 1835-1935'. (see page 36)

The artists who had, in these years, given Great Western publicity this much-needed fillip, continued to produce a steady flow of new posters between the centenary and the outbreak of the second war. Among newcomers, Ronald Lampitt's three paintings in the form of a mosaic, for Devon, Cornwall and the Cotswolds, were particularly novel and effective. A poster of Windsor Castle issued in 1932 was by a member of the publicity staff, Charles H. J. Mayo, who had joined the department from the traffic side in 1931. In addition to doing much of the art work for posters and other publicity matter, he produced perhaps the best-known of all Great Western posters, 'Speed to the West', issued just before the war, and used as the frontispiece to this book.

A considerable amount of art work was done for the GWR in the 1930s by a firm of artists' agents, Ralph & Mott, who employed a team of artists whose work can be found on many Great Western posters, folders and booklets under the pseudonym Ralph Mott. Though not all in the very top class, their work did play a considerable part in enlivening GWR publicity at this time, and some artists who achieved prominence in later years acquired valuable experience while working for the firm.

The quality of pictorial posters was not only dependent upon the artists who painted the original pictures. Until the advent of photo-lithography in the later 1930s, the designs had to be copied on to stone by lithographic artists at the printers, with an inevitable loss of the original artist's touch. The quality of the paper, too, could seriously affect the finished poster, so that economy in printing, always the watchword of the stationery department and its superintendent, W. H. Jarvis, not infrequently resulted in disappointing reproduction.

One of the difficulties constantly faced by the publicity department was the allocation of the very limited expenditure to the many different facilities offered by the railway. In press advertising, something like fifty per cent was devoted to excursions and cheap trips; by far the larger number of sale publications consisted

of guides aimed at attracting holiday traffic, and the majority of
pictorial posters, as we have seen, served the same function. By
the time these needs had been met there was little money left for
all the ancillary services which the railway provided—restaurant
cars, season tickets, parcels and luggage facilities, to name but a
few. When the Great Western did at last turn to first-rate artists
for its posters, these were almost entirely employed to publicise
the holiday areas, and posters for specialised services were generally of a low standard.

It was only in the 1930s that the company, under pressure from
road competition, began to advertise the many potentially lucrative
sidelines, many of which were largely unknown to the
general public, and at this time, too, the hitherto neglected
goods department was at last given a larger share of advertising
expenditure.

Production of pictorial posters reached a peak in the 1930s.
Some 50,000 were issued in 1932, and this figure doubled in 1934,
after which there was a gradual falling-off in numbers, with
57,000 produced in 1939.

From 1940 to 1946 the hoardings were bereft of their accustomed gaiety, the colourful posters of the railway companies being
superseded by government propaganda and by such unnatural
slogans as 'Is Your Journey Really Necessary?' But in 1947 there
was a welcome return of pictorial advertising as the railways
braced themselves for the post-war boom in holidays by rail—a
boom which soon passed once motor cars became more plentiful
and petrol rationing was abolished.

The posters of the twilight year before nationalisation followed
the general trend of the later pre-war designs, with the Frank
Newbould style much in evidence. The use of Gill Sans lettering
and the roundel, introduced before the war, gave to this last series
of Great Western posters a freshness and simplicity which was
greatly appreciated by a public weary of wartime drabness. With
the title-panel removed, many were framed to decorate station
waiting rooms, and some of them, faded with long exposure to
sunlight, remained for many years as a reminder of the frustrated
post-war plans of the Great Western Railway.

BOOKLETS AND FOLDERS

A substantial part of the publicity output of the Great Western consisted of a miscellaneous assortment of booklets, mostly illustrated, which were distributed free of charge. They form perhaps the most interesting class of the company's publications, covering as they do many of the wide range of specialised services both for passenger and goods traffic, as well as supplementing the larger travel books in the never-ending campaign to attract holiday traffic to the line. And if the subjects were varied, the treatment and style of these booklets were even more diverse.

GREAT WESTERN RAILWAY

Of England.

Handbook for Travellers from Over Seas.

Cover of 56-page booklet issued in 1912

One of the earliest, and possibly the very first, is dated 1903, ante-dating the first sale publication by a year. This was a 56-page booklet with a coloured cover and half-tone illustrations of Great

Western scenery, and it carried the self-conscious title of *Great Western Railway Illustrated Pamphlet*. Among other early booklets was one issued in 1908 to mark the first call of the SS *Lanfranc* (Booth Line) at Fishguard on 2 April of that year. This retold the story of the attempted French invasion at Fishguard in 1797, and the text was illustrated with a curious mixture of reproductions of old prints and photographs of a Great Western steamer, a boat train and the Fishguard Bay Hotel. A year later the company issued *From Severn Sea to the German Ocean*, to advertise the Direct Route from South Wales to East Anglia via Cheltenham, Stratford-upon-Avon, the LNWR and Great Eastern.

Follow the Sun by the Holiday Line, published in 1911, foreshadowed the *Through the Window* series of the mid-1920s. This 56-page booklet contained coloured route maps of lines from Paddington to the West of England, interspersed with hotel advertisements. Its avowed purpose was to 'answer any reasonable enquiry *en route* upon matters topographical'.

The first publicity matter specifically designed for America appeared well before the 1914 war. *A Handbook for Travellers from Over Seas* contained topographical notes and information on Great Western services, and was issued in July 1912, while a year later *Attractive Tours by Rail and Automobile* listed trips specially selected for American visitors by GWR trains and road motors (here, appropriately, re-named automobiles). Continental visitors were not forgotten, and in 1913 two illustrated booklets *La Belle Angleterre* and *Englands Landschafts-Perlen*, were issued for French and German consumption. After the first war the company considerably increased its overseas publicity; in 1932 no less than 385,000 folders and booklets were sent abroad, chiefly to America, Canada, France and Germany, and in the same year literature was issued in Swedish. In co-operation with Mitteleuropaisches Reiseburo a booklet in German illustrating Great Western scenery was printed in Berlin. This was entirely a German production, but there was something very familiar inside the back cover—the ubiquitous Emery Walker GWR route map.

Between the wars an annual illustrated booklet briefly describing 'the GWR holiday lands' and giving general travel information, appeared under the simple title *Holidays*. Popular areas such as the West Country and the Cotswolds were dealt with in separate, well-illustrated booklets. Maxwell Fraser wrote a number of these, including *Smiling Somerset* and *The West Country* (1931), and *The Cotswold Country* (1936), and also four small county gazetteers for American visitors (1931-2). These latter, like a good many of the earlier booklets, had dull and rather uninviting covers, but in the later 1930s these gave way to brighter designs, including some very striking covers by Frank Newbould for *Windsor* (1937) and Maxwell Fraser's *London* (1939), for which he also did a series of sketches to supplement the gravure plates.

The popularity of camping and rambling led the company to produce annual booklets in the later 30s with some attractive coloured covers and containing detailed directories of camping

4-page leaflet, 1932

sites, with rail travel facilities and cartage services for camping equipment, and an annual series of booklets giving information on its own camping coaches commenced in 1934.

Souvenir booklets were issued for Land Cruises which were instituted in 1931, and one passenger enjoyed her cruise so much that she wrote an account of it which was published by the company as *Impressions of my Land Cruise* in 1929.

On the goods side, the principal publication was the 142-page *Guide to Economical Transport*, issued in 1936 to replace an earlier book *How to Send and How to Save*. The *Guide* gave details of services (including, rather surprisingly, all those delightful nicknames given to the regular long-distance goods trains), latest times of acceptance for goods, and delivery times, as well as full information on such matters as containers, COD, farm and furniture removals, livestock traffic and private sidings. Special booklets were issued for the Railhead Distribution Scheme, introduced in 1926, and country cartage door-to-door services were covered by an illustrated booklet of which the 1935 edition had a particularly clever and effective cover by 'Ralph Mott'.

Immense numbers and varieties of booklet were produced by the Great Western over the years. They ranged from reduced fares pamphlets of a mere eight pages to elaborate and well-printed brochures for the company's hotels, from pocket-size lists of agricultural shows to picture guides to winter resorts. They poured forth from the publicity department in endless succession. Four hundred thousand were distributed in the UK alone in 1931, and in centenary year booklets and folders totalled one and a half million. Over the years, tens of millions must have been despatched from the stationery warehouse at Paddington to stations, travel agents, business and industrial firms and individuals. Many would be picked up, glanced at and thrown away, but some, no doubt, persuaded someone, somewhere, to hire a camping coach, to move his furniture by container, or to build a factory on the Great Western. The trouble was that the department had very little idea of the effectiveness of all this printed matter. As G. E. Orton said, 'we have to have considerable faith'.

The illustrated folder, which made its appearance a few years before the first war, filled a gap in publicity between the traditional handbill, used mainly for excursions and cheap trips, and the substantial travel books which were being issued from Paddington from 1904 onwards. The early folders dealt with specific services —through cross-country trains, road motors, two-hour trains to Birmingham, the Fishguard route to Ireland—or offered suggestions for holiday travel—Week-ends in the West, Up-River Holidays, Inland Health Resorts, and so on. (See page 53)

Printed on good quality paper, with colourful covers, they contained in addition to timetables and fares, a good spread of photographs and enough descriptive matter to whet the appetite of the prospective passenger. The folders gave an altogether more attractive impression than the rather dreary handbill, and they marked an important step forward in the development of railway advertising. Rough layouts were prepared in the advertising department, but the final design was left to the printers, and some of the early folders, notably those printed by Petty & Sons Ltd of Reading, were distinctive and generally well produced.

After the fashion of the day, the half-tone reproductions of the photographs were very small—a fault found also in the early travel books, but by the mid 20s these gave way to larger reproductions. Up to this time photographs were commonly used on the covers in conjunction with colour letterpress, but these, too, had disappeared by about 1930. Many of the designs from this period were unsigned, a few carry the signatures of well-known artists like Warwick Goble and Frank Newbould, while others were designed in the publicity department, whose head of production, Arthur Sawyer, designed some of the covers. From 1934 Ralph & Mott's studio provided the designs for several series of folders which followed the same trends as the pictorial posters of the period and, like the latter, began to carry the roundel monogram from 1931, in which year some 650,000 folders were distributed in this country.

Not all the publicity material turned out from Paddington was issued solely in the cause of the Great Western. Combined advertising campaigns with resorts had long been the company's policy, and indeed many of the folders for holiday areas carried only the minimum of railway advertising. In the later 30s folders bearing the names of the Great Western and LMS, and a series for distribution abroad carrying the Associated British and Irish Railways monogram were produced at Paddington.

At this time much of the descriptive matter in the folders was written by Maxwell Fraser, whose encyclopaedic knowledge of 'The Western Land', and her very readable style, were a great asset to the publicity department.

It hardly needs to be said that the major part of this output was, as in other forms of publicity, devoted to the traditional holiday areas served by the Great Western, but there were very many other subjects upon which folders were issued, ranging from holiday season tickets and Land Cruises to Air Services, motor car transit and luggage arrangements. It has already been mentioned that goods services were increasingly prominent in the company's publicity in the 1930s, and some very attractive literature on goods facilities was issued, for some of which Frank Newbould designed the covers. Here, too, the staff at Paddington was responsible for the layout and production of joint publicity material for the four group companies, of which very large quantities were produced. In 1938 alone 2,200,000 goods traffic folders were printed.

A series of folders with very well-designed covers by 'Ralph Mott' was issued in 1939 dealing with such matters as insurance of livestock, COD, refrigerated and insulated transport, and door-to-door containers. There was a freshness and originality about these goods folders in which it could be said that this part of Great Western publicity reached its zenith. Perhaps so many years devoted to extolling the charms of the Cornish Riviera had exhausted the supply of new ideas, and the publicity staff turned with unaccustomed enthusiasm to the problems of persuading industry to 'Go Great Western'.

Chapter 4

Sale Publications

The Great Western Railway was always known, and often admired, for its individuality, from Brunel's Broad Gauge and the Swindon tapered boiler to the insistence that Tickets Must be Shewn.

One of the minor oddities of the Great Western was its successful and sustained activities as a book publisher extending over more than forty years. Millions of GWR publications, varying from small threepenny booklets to the beautifully produced series on cathedrals, abbeys and castles, were sold between 1904 and 1947, and though the purely nominal prices precluded any hope of a financial profit, the indirect effect must have been considerable, both in terms of actual traffic and in prestige. In this respect the company was ahead of its time in putting so much faith in prestige advertising, but there is no doubting the wisdom of this policy.

These sale publications, to give them their official name, were quite unique in British publishing; holiday guides and other travel publications were issued at various times by most railway companies, or were published by commercial publishers with the companies' approval, but no other railway achieved anything near the output or quality of the Great Western's publications, and it is therefore important that something should be said about this side of the publicity department's activities. There is, today, a greater interest in the minor forms of travel literature than formerly, and to assist those who are forming a collection of the GWR books a check-list is given in the appendix.

The first book published by the company, appropriately, was

The Cornish Riviera, which appeared early in 1904, and heralded a series of uniform volumes covering various parts of the Great Western system. These were written by A. M. Broadley, a prolific historical writer of the day. As in almost all the early Great Western books, no author's name appeared on the title-page. There followed in July of the same year *Historic Sites and Scenes of England*, intended mainly for American visitors, and during the next five years volumes on North and South Wales, Devon, Southern Ireland and Rural London appeared at intervals, all priced at threepence in paper covers. A larger book, *Wonderful Wessex* was published in June 1908 at sixpence ($2\frac{1}{2}$p).

All Broadley's books had a very large sale indeed, and successive reprints and new editions appeared until as late as 1926, by which time they had become distinctly dated and were allowed to go out of print. *The Cornish Riviera*, described by one reviewer as 'the last word in art in railway advertising' ran into five editions and over 250,000 copies of the first edition alone were sold. The books first appeared printed entirely on art paper, with the small half-tone illustrations incorporated in the text, but after the first war the high cost of art paper led to the text being printed on an antique paper with the plates, some of them enlarged, printed separately. The texts were revised at almost every printing, and later editions had large folding maps of the GWR system.

These books were considered to be of sufficient permanent value to be issued in an attractive cloth board binding with gilt lettering, the price of which was 2s 6d ($12\frac{1}{2}$p). Great Western travel books were not only in demand as leisure reading; the 1908 *Holiday Haunts* contains an advertisement which quotes the Clerk to Reading Educational Committee in praise of their value in teaching geography and history in schools.

The early editions had hotel and other advertisements at the end, as well as Great Western timetables and information about fares, routes and tours. Needless to say, a list of the company's other publications appeared in each volume. Advertising by outside bodies was arranged either direct with the company or through the Great Western's advertising agent, Wills Ltd of Cannon Street. When the series was revised after the war only GWR advertising matter was retained, and this on a much reduced

G.W.R. SERIES OF ⸺
⸺ TRAVEL BOOKS

"The Literature of Locomotion."—*Vide* THE OBSERVER.

The series of travel books published by the G.W.R., of which this volume is one, have become widely known as "The Holiday Books of the Holiday Line." They have been described as unique in railway literature, and form an exceedingly popular series of literary handbooks. All the travel books are illustrated, and each contains a map. ⸺

LIST OF TRAVEL BOOKS.

THE CORNISH RIVIERA. Price 3d., post free 6d.
"The admirable pictures and brightly written letterpress well fulfil their purpose of explaining how to get to this national resort, and what to see there."
—*Daily Telegraph.*

SOUTHERN IRELAND : ITS LAKES AND LANDSCAPES. Price 3d., post free 6d.
"Both dainty and artistic. . . . Fully illustrated by reproductions of charming photographs."—*Madame.*

RURAL LONDON : The Chalfont Country and the Thames Valley. Price 3d., post free 6d.

THE CATHEDRAL LINE OF ENGLAND. Its sacred Sites and Shrines. Price 3d., post free 6d.
"A neat and comprehensive brochure, detailing the numerous cathedrals, abbeys, shrines, and sacred sites within easy reach on the Great Western Railway system."
—*Daily Graphic.*

HISTORIC SITES AND SCENES OF ENGLAND. For Travellers of all Nations. Price 3d., post free 6d.

SOUTH WALES : THE COUNTRY OF CASTLES. Price 3d., post free 6d.
"A most interesting book. . . Details, in a very comprehensive manner, the undoubted 'beauties of South Wales.'"
—*The Tatler.*

WONDERFUL WESSEX : Wilts, Somerset and Dorset. Price 6d., post free 10d.
"Most comprehensive and splendidly illustrated . . invaluable to tourists. The Great Western Railway Company is to be congratulated upon the production of so complete a guide.'—*Daily Mirror.*

NORTH WALES : The British Tyrol. Price 3d., post free 6d.

HOMES FOR ALL : London's West rn Borderlands. A residential guide and property register. Issued quarterly. Free. Postage 3d.

The travel books may be obtained at the Company's principal stations and offices at the prices shewn, or will be forwarded on application to the office of Mr. C. ALDINGTON, Superintendent of the Line, G.W.R., PADDINGTON STATION, LONDON, W., on receipt of stamps. ⸺

THE HOLIDAY BOOKS ⸺
...OF...
⸺ THE HOLIDAY LINE.

Advertisement for sale publications in the 1912 edition of *The Cornish Riviera* scale, usually no more than a page or two devoted to other publications.

Broadley's books contain little of purely railway interest, but the occasional photograph of an early GWR road motor in a Cornish village, or a 'Star' hauling the 'Limited' on the sea wall at Dawlish, remind the reader of the pre-1914 Great Western, while in the text the opportunity was usually taken to remind readers of new developments on 'The Holiday Line', as in the introduction to the 1907 edition of *South Wales,* where mention is made of the working of the Manchester & Milford Railway by the GWR, and in *Rural London* (1909) where the then new GW-GC joint line to High Wycombe, 'traversing . . . the ancient Perivale Forest and the uplands of Park Royal' was alluded to.

The last of this pioneer series was *Beautiful Brittany,* published in 1909 and revised a year later. The intention here was clearly to encourage the use of the company's Plymouth—Brest steamers, inaugurated in 1907, as well as the trains to Plymouth. *Southern Ireland* (1904) was likewise issued with an eye to publicising the steamer service from New Milford, soon to be replaced by the new Fishguard—Rosslare service which commenced in 1906.

A. M. Broadley's success as a travel writer was not matched by his attempt to write a history of the Great Western. In 1911 the appearance in the Paddington offices of proof copies of *All About the Great Western,* written by Broadley, caused some concern among senior officers, and although a considerable amount of money had already been spent on blocks and type-setting, the book was abandoned.

Publishing activity up to the first war was confined almost entirely to the Broadley series, apart from a smaller booklet, *Cornwall and its Wild Life* and a useful *Haunts and Hints for Anglers,* written by the editor of a popular angling periodical, which appeared in 1914. During the war publishing ceased altogether except for a new edition of Broadley's *Devon: The Shire of the Sea Kings,* published in 1916.

There is, however, an important publication from the pre-war era which many would regard today as of much greater interest than the travel books. This is the small booklet *Names of Engines* which first appeared in 1911 at sixpence a copy. To be strictly accurate, this, and subsequent editions before 1932, were published by the *Great Western Railway Magazine*, and not by the company as such, but since the *Magazine* by that time was owned by the company, they were for all practical purposes in the same category as the other GWR publications.

Here again the Great Western was breaking new ground, for no other company had produced a similar work on its locomotive stock. Information about the building of new engines, and other details of interest to railway enthusiasts had been given in the *Magazine* from as early as 1904, but such had been the demand from readers that a separate publication was clearly needed. The task of compiling it fell to Arthur J. L. White, of the Chief Mechanical Engineer's office at Swindon, who became chief clerk in 1920 and died in 1929 only two years after completing a long series of articles about the works in the *Magazine*, extending over a period of sixteen years.

Sales were such that a new edition appeared in 1914 and another during the war, in 1917. Under slightly varying titles, the engine book appeared periodically until 1946. From 1932 onwards *The GWR Engines Book* was produced by the publicity department, and it was given a new, pictorial cover and the text was rearranged and enlarged. By 1938, when W. G. Chapman took over the editorship, the 24-page booklet of 1911 had grown to a profusely illustrated volume of 112 pages.

No new sale publications appeared after the war until 1922, by which time Pole was in the general manager's chair at Paddington. In the field of book publishing, as in other spheres, the company made rapid strides during his regime. That this was due both to Pole's general keenness on publicity and to his particular appreciation of the value of the indirect approach (he used the word propaganda) is certain. Between 1923 and 1929 some notable titles were added to the fast-growing list, in which quantity was more than matched by quality.

In 1922 a short book by E. A. Pratt, *The War Record of the Great Western Railway*, made its appearance. This was based on his general work on the railways' contribution to the 1914-18 conflict, *British Railways and the Great War*, which had appeared in two volumes in the previous year. Pratt, who was a leading authority on railway history and economics, inserted some additional material into the Great Western book, which was published by Selwyn & Blount and distributed by the *Magazine* at one shilling.

In the same year the company produced a series of 48 leaflets on the legends of the West Country by G. B. Barham, under the pseudonym of 'Lyonesse', which were reissued later in the year as the first two of four little sixpenny booklets entitled *Legend Land*. Printed at the Ballantyne Press, they had ornamental initial letters in addition to the line drawings which illustrated each legend, and were certainly productions of a high quality, foreshadowing some much larger books in the same style which were soon to appear. The third and fourth volumes of *Legend Land*, uniform in style but printed by Kelly & Kelly, followed in 1923. A small number of sets were attractively bound in white leather for presentation.

Nothing of note appeared from the publicity section at the time of the grouping. The only publication directly resulting from the Railways Act was a 48-page book *The Cambrian Coast* which was produced well in time for the 1923 holiday season to encourage the use of the Cambrian Railways' lines acquired by the GWR. August 1923 saw the beginning of a new series of cheap but well illustrated books for railway enthusiasts—young and old. The author was Walter George Chapman, a member of the general manager's staff who joined the Great Western in 1896. In 1908 he was awarded one of the first three I. K. Brunel Medals for the most successful student in the railway department of the London School of Economics. While in the general manager's office he wrote four books in the series 'For Boys of All Ages', and after being transferred to the publicity department in 1929 produced three more as well as editing the *Engines Book*.

The first title in the series was *The 10.30 Limited*, and as was to be expected, sales of such a well-produced book on such a popular subject, modestly priced at a shilling (5p), were phenomenal. Seventy-one thousand copies were sold in six months, and of the first four of Chapman's books some 130,000 found their way into the hands of grateful 'boys of all ages'. By 1934 three of the first four titles had gone out of print and *Cheltenham Flyer* was

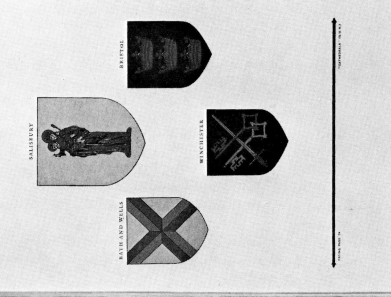

Page 89: *Chapter opening from* Cathedrals, 1924, *showing ornamental initial and plate of arms in gold and colours*

WINCHESTER CATHEDRAL

HE Cathedral Church of the Holy Trinity is so enwrapped in the history of Winchester—at one time supreme in England—as to call for some brief reference to the infancy of the city itself. The white chalk hills which embosom Winchester suggest the name "Caer Gwent" (the White City), given to the town by the Celts. It may perhaps have meant "a market town." It was certainly a town before the Romans came. To the Romans, who occupied it about the middle of the first century A.D., it became known as Venta Belgarum, and to the Saxons as Wintonceaster. There are many absurd legends as to the early history of the city. Even the British King Arthur is said to have been connected with it; and the mediæval "Round Table," now in the castle, was supposed to date from his time. It was repaired for Henry VIII. Of the Roman period traces were discovered in the course of excavations for the castle which was intended for Charles II, when coins of Constantine the Great were unearthed; since then portions of mosaic pavements and more coins have been found.

Camden, in his "Britannia," tells how, in the Saxon Heptarchy, the West Saxon kings lived in the city "and adorned it with magnificent churches and an episcopal see." There is no doubt that the city exercised a great and beneficent influence on the growth of Christianity in the south of England. T. E. Warton in his fascinating book (1760), "A Description of the City and College and Cathedral of Winchester," says that under King Athelstan Winchester had six mints for the coinage of money. Edgar set forth that the standard weights and measures should be "such as is observed at London and at Winchester." Egbert, when crowned King of all Britain, made it a centre of learning which attracted such scholars as St. Grimbald and Asser, of St. David's. It was here that the Anglo-Saxon Chronicle was written. Cnut made it his seat of government, while Edward the Confessor was crowned in the minster founded by Alfred, just to the north of the site of the Cathedral.

The short distance between Winchester and Southampton led William the Conqueror to make the city his capital also, and, as in Saxon times, the royal treasure was kept there, for we read that at the Conqueror's death Rufus hastened to seize it. The city became exceedingly prosperous in the twelfth century as one of the first centres of the woollen trade, and many traders were attracted hither by the establishment of St. Giles's Fair by William II in a charter to Walkelin. In the time of King Stephen and the Empress Matilda Winchester suffered much by fire. Richard Cœur de Lion was crowned a second time at the Cathedral after his ransom. Henry III, who was born at Winchester, often spent Christmas there. As a seat of government Winchester began to wane during his reign, and the prosperity of the city to

24

HOLIDAY HAUNTS

Season—1924.

Health and Pleasure Resorts, Hotels,
Boarding Houses, Seaside and
Country Lodgings, Farmhouses.

ENGLAND, WALES
——— and ———
CHANNEL ISLANDS

[6d.]

Page 90 (above left) *Cover of the first issue of* Holiday Haunts, *1906, printed in grey, dark blue and white;* (right) *standard cover used from 1911 to 1928;* (below left) Holiday Haunts *in its later and brighter garb, 1932;* (right) *the* Holiday Haunts *bookmarkers issued in the 1920s*

written and published in that year to replace them. Although sales of this 240-page book (still at 1s) were not so high as in the case of the first of the series, it still ran into three editions, totalling 30,000 copies, in six months.

In 1932 Chapman left the publicity department to take charge of the GWR Central Enquiry Bureau. While there he wrote the last two of the books by which he is remembered by many friends of the Great Western Railway, *Track Topics* (1935) and *Loco's of "The Royal Road"* (1936). In his foreword to his last book Chapman revealed that it was the Prince of Wales (later Duke of Windsor) who used this title for the Great Western in his speech at the centenary banquet in 1935.

The most ambitious publishing venture so far made its appearance seven months after Chapman's first book. Not only was the subject completely different, but so was the treatment. Sir Felix Pole tells in his memoirs of the events leading to the publication by the GWR of a book on the cathedrals situated on the company's system.

George E. Beer, at one time News Editor of *The Times*, had joined the Great Western as a publicity and propaganda adviser to Pole, but after only a year or two he was appointed News Editor of the *Daily Mail*. He seems to have acquired some affection for the Great Western during his short stay, and as a tribute to the company he offered to write a book on cathedrals. The offer was accepted, the manuscript was approved by the Deans of the cathedrals included in the book, and the Archbishop of Canterbury was invited to contribute a foreword.

By any standards, *Cathedrals* was a fine book. Great care was taken with the typography, which was supervised by W. G. Tucker, and the book was printed on Abbey Mills antique laid paper by the Ballantyne Press. The plates, in sepia gravure, and the reproductions of heraldic shields in gold, silver and colours, completed a most satisfactory blend of traditional typography and modern reproduction processes. *Cathedrals* was published in March 1924 in paper covers at 2s 6d ($12\frac{1}{2}$p) and, in July 1925, in quarter-cloth boards at 5s (25p). Apart from a folding pictorial map, discreetly placed in a pocket at the end of the book, which was added to the second edition, there was no

F

CHAPTER THE THIRD

"CORNISH RIVIERA EXPRESS"

ONGRATULATIONS on your punctuality, for I see our three-faced friend above says exactly 10.15. For the next six or seven hours I want you to keep your eyes and ears open and I think I can promise that you will see and hear much of interest on your favourite subject.

There was a motive in getting you here at this time, and I thought, before setting out on our own journey, we might have a look at the " Cornish Riviera Express," now standing at the platform. Personally, I always get a thrill from the departure of " the 10.30 " which leaves this platform daily on its wonderful run at high speed to our most westerly town of Penzance—a run without a pause for breath until it reaches Plymouth (226 miles distant) in four hours.

Chapter opening from Cheltenham Flyer, 1934

advertising matter of any kind.

Cathedrals was an instant success, as it deserved to be. The first edition of 30,000 was soon sold and a second, of 10,000 copies, appeared in July of the following year, with a 20,000 reprint seven months later. Reviewers were full of praise, and when King George V and Queen Mary were presented with a copy after their visit to Swindon works on 28 April 1924 the Queen immediately asked for more copies.

No sooner had *Cathedrals* appeared than planning began for a companion volume on abbeys. For this work, Dr M. R. James, Provost of Eton, a widely respected scholar (and writer of ghost stories) was the author, and the book, in the same style as its predecessor but rather larger, was again printed at the Ballantyne Press and published in August 1925. Only a bound edition of 20,000 copies, was issued, and a second impression of the same size was needed within six months. In 1926 the trilogy was completed with Sir Charles Oman's *Castles,* an even larger book running to some 232 pages.

It is a tribute to the choice of authors as well as to the high quality of design and printing of these books that after more than forty years they are still admired, and *Castles* in particular is regarded as an important contribution to its subject and shows every sign of becoming quite difficult to find in the second-hand bookshops.

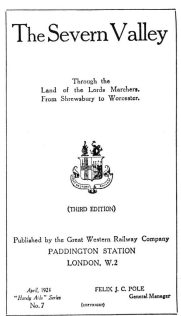

Title-page of *Handy Aids* series

During the 1920s a very large number of small illustrated booklets describing the Great Western tourist areas was distributed. These were the 'Handy Aids' series, comprising eleven titles, most of which ran into several editions. Publicity department announce-

THE VALE OF RHEIDOL RAILWAY.

TO reach Devil's Bridge over the Falls of the Rheidol take the narrow-gauge railway called the "Vale of Rheidol Branch." How interesting sound the names of the stations from Aberystwyth:Llanbadarn, Glanrafon, Capel Bangor, Nantyronen, Aberffrwd, Rheidol Falls, Rhiwfron, Devil's Bridge. The hour it takes to go up by rail is, on a fine summer or autumn day, an hour of delight. Everything there is to be seen can be seen. On some mountain railways the trees hamper the view; here the eye ranges unobstructed over the valley, and the splendid condition of the line and of the trains makes the journey easy as well as pleasant. In August as many as five thousand passengers make the journey in a week.

The first stages of the railway ride from Aberystwyth are not very remarkable. The dignified National Library is very noticeable on leaving the town. There is the winding Rheidol, and then great gorse-covered patches which, when in flower, are all glorious—not just a bush or two, but enough to cover a couple of acres. Some twenty minutes are taken to travel through this more level part of the journey, but it is never dull. After passing Capel Bangor the mountains appear on the left, and soon the climb of a hundred feet of rise for every mile of the journey begins. At one point near here the river bend appears to enclose a large island. A delightful view up and down the valley

Chapter opening from Welsh Mountain Railways, 1924

ments in *Holiday Haunts* referred to them quaintly as 'dainty little volumes'; they were in fact well printed and included a large folding map of the GWR, but were marred by small duotone plates, considered artistic at the time. The texts were adapted by the publicity department staff from Broadley's larger books. No charge was made for the 'Handy Aids' series, but they were always advertised with the sale publications and by their contents as well as their format are more closely related to the latter than to the free folders and other direct publicity matter. This also applies to a similar series of free booklets issued in the same period which included *The Glories of the Thames, Inland & Marine Spas,* and *Welsh Mountain Railways.* This last title, issued in May 1924, is something of a typographical curiosity. It was printed by George W. Jones, a well-known craft printer and type-designer, in a style more fitted to a private press book than a railway publicity booklet. How the production of this particular booklet came to be entrusted to this eminent printer remains a mystery.

Copies of these free booklets, and many of the sale publications, were from time to time issued in crimson cloth or leather bindings, with the GWR arms in gilt, for presentation or for use in hotels, clubs and ships. The binding cases were merely glued onto the existing paper covers and were quite distinct from the truly bound versions of some titles which were available for sale.

W. H. Jarvis, the superintendent of the stationery and printing department from 1919 to 1942, was interested in printing history and typography, and wrote two articles on the subject in the *Magazine* in 1931. The excellent, if somewhat consciously antique, typography of many publications may owe something to his taste.

The publicity department had another short series in hand in 1924, and this time it was something for the actual railway passenger. *Through the Window: Paddington to Penzance,* gave a mile-by-mile commentary on the scenery unfolded through the carriage window, and opposite each page of text, which had small sketches of prominent features, was a large-scale strip map showing a section of the line and surrounding country. Unlike almost all Great Western books, the 'Through the Window' series was compiled and produced for the company by an outside firm, Edward J. Burrow & Co Ltd of Cheltenham. Burrows were, and still are, specialists in guide books and other topographical publishing, and their books were well above average in production and design. The three volumes in this series were no exception. The second title, *Paddington to Birkenhead,* appeared in 1925, and *Paddington to Killarney* (via Fishguard) a year later. All were priced at one shilling (5p) in stiff card covers. If the present writer may be allowed a personal note here, it is appropriate that this account of GWR publicity is being written in a building once occupied by Messrs Burrows, and in a room overlooking the drawing office where the 'Through the Window' books were designed.

New editions of the early books by A. M. Broadley, and a whole host of minor booklets kept the department fully occupied all through the 1920s, but in 1927 the company published by far the most ambitious, not to say most useful, book that ever came out of Paddington—the *History of the Great Western Railway.*

This book was the outcome of Sir Felix Pole's interest in Great Western history acquired in the course of his earlier literary activities with the *Magazine* and in free-lance journalism. Some material had already been gathered by the head of the telegraph office at Bristol, George Milford, and this was taken over by E. T. MacDermot, a barrister and admirer of the GWR. MacDermot was given every facility to extract from the company's records all the facts he required to write a comprehensive history. He was assisted by E. L. Ahrons and A. C. W. Lowe who compiled the chapters on locomotives and rolling stock. The whole work is not only a tribute to MacDermot's painstaking research, in which his legal training was invaluable, but also a model of its kind. It was published in two volumes, the first, which appeared in 1927, being in two parts. The second volume was published in 1931. The illustrations were provided by the publicity department and the stationery and printing department was responsible for production. As befitted such an important work, an outstanding book printer, the Chiswick Press, was given the printing contract.

In the years after the second world war MacDermot's *History* became increasingly scarce and expensive and it was with great pleasure that students of railway history greeted the revised edition prepared by Mr C. R. Clinker, himself an old Great Western man who had assisted MacDermot in preparing his material, in 1964.

Between publication of the first and second volumes of the *History* the company published, in 1929, a portfolio of twelve gravure plates of GWR engines, suitable for framing. This was very good value at a shilling (5p), but sales were not very brisk and the

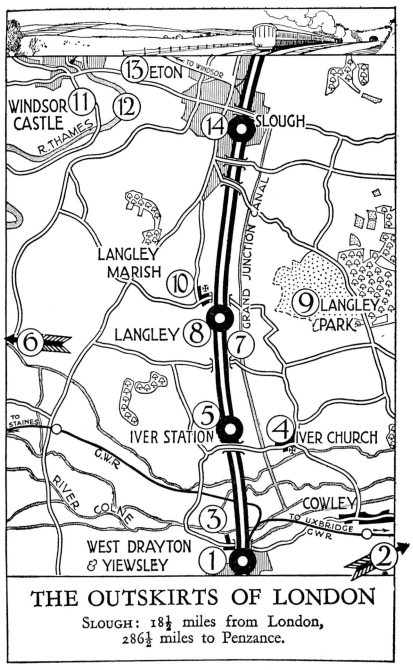

THE OUTSKIRTS OF LONDON
SLOUGH: 18½ miles from London,
286½ miles to Penzance.

Strip route map from *Through the Window: Paddington to Penzance*, 1924.
The numerals refer the reader to the text on the opposite page

price was reduced to sixpence (2½p) in 1932.

The disappearance of the familiar white-covered books by A. M. Broadley, for so long the mainstay of the Great Western book list, left a gap which needed to be filled if the attractions of the resorts of the West Country and Wales were to be kept in the public eye. The task of writing a new book on the Cornish Riviera and a companion volume on Devon was given to the popular and prolific travel writer, S. P. B. Mais, who, it is interesting to note, had then recently written a free booklet for the Southern Railway called *My Finest Holiday*.

The Cornish Riviera and *Glorious Devon* appeared in August 1928. The style and format were completely different from the books of similar titles of twenty years earlier. The dignified but rather dull white covers and the over-small half-tone illustrations gave way to bright, boldly coloured covers, cut flush in the style of the modern paperback, and up-to-date photographs reproduced as full-page gravure plates, while in the text were pleasing pen and ink sketches. The type used was Garamond, first used by the Great Western in *The 10.30 Limited* and later employed in many of the company's books. The price of these attractive and eye-catching volumes was the now traditional shilling. There was also a cloth-bound version which sold for a modest 2s 6d (12½p). Garamond has, appropriately, been used in the present book, though without the decorative ligatured characters ct and st which are a feature of the version used by the GWR.

The first printings of 10,000 copies of each title both quickly sold, and new editions were needed in the following April. The onset of the industrial depression in 1929 had a substantial effect on the company's passenger revenue which was reflected in the reduced sales of these books, and not until June 1932 were reprints again needed. A third, revised edition of both titles was issued in February 1934 and they were still being advertised in *Holiday Haunts* as late as 1940. The last edition was distinguished by new covers designed by the eminent artist E. McKnight Kauffer, whose rather limited contribution to Great Western publicity has already been mentioned. It is significant that sales never approached those of the Broadley series which appeared when this kind of publication was a novelty.

It might be said that these two books introduced a new look in Great Western publications which was also exemplified in the 1929 *Holiday Haunts*, which for the first time also had a bright coloured flush-cut cover, and this brighter presentation became the accepted standard in the publicity department's future output. This general refurbishing was the crowning achievement of W. H. Fraser's seven years as publicity agent. He retired at the end of 1931 leaving a department every bit as efficient and progressive as its counterparts in the other group companies.

A distinguished travel writer, whose name will always be associated with Macmillan's *Highways and Byways* series, A. G. Bradley, wrote one book for the Great Western, and this was published in 1930. *Pembrokeshire and South West Wales* was not only by a first class author, but was also claimed to be the first book published for general sale to be set in Bruce Rogers' beautiful Centaur type.

While the changing typography and illustration of the company's publications reflected the fashion of the day, the subject matter too can be seen as a reflection of changing habits in holidays and leisure activities generally. The formal fortnight by the sea at Torquay or Aberystwyth was giving way in the 1930s, at least among the younger generation, to such pursuits as camping, hiking and caravanning. These less costly forms of relaxation gained great favour during the years of the depression when many families found conventional holidays too expensive, and in the early 30s the Great Western Railway used some ingenuity to attract passenger traffic of new kinds to compensate for the reduction in the number of normal holidaymakers. Camping coaches, introduced in 1934, Hikers' Specials and Mystery Trains (1932) and many new reduced fares all helped to improve passenger receipts. The publicity department was deeply involved in all this and embarked upon a series of books for hikers and ramblers, written by Hugh E. Page and E. Roland Williams. Page was the secretary of the North Finchley Rambling Club, and a great champion of the traditional rights of walkers over field paths. He personally undertook all the walks described in his books and was killed in an accident while indulging in his favourite pursuit. Well supplied with sketch maps and line illustrations, the first volume, *Rambles in the Chiltern Country,* appeared in 1931. It had to be reprinted within a month of publication, and ran into two more editions by 1937. Further titles covered the

THE

QUANTOCKS

CHAPTER III

In some curious way, the Quantocks impress even the casual visitor with their air of rich contentment. It is not merely that nature has been prodigal in her gifts to this lovely, fertile range of hills, but that an air of happy serenity penetrates to every village, and climbs to the heights where long stretches of heather and bracken seem as fresh and untouched as in the days when the world was young. There is an atmosphere which suggests the fullness of contentment which we associate with the spacious days of Elizabeth, when England could lay just claim to the title of " merry," and quaint customs and age-old traditions were maintained as a matter of course. Whilst so much of the rest of England is being modernised, life flows on among these lovely hills with a placidity born of prosperity and quiet content. Rich manor houses, fine old farms, and charming cottages, are to be seen, but no factories, or even towns, to disturb the suggestion of ancient peace and plenty.

Chapter opening from Maxwell Fraser's *Somerset,* 1934

popular holiday areas served by the GWR. In all, seven rambling books appeared and some were reissued during the second war when many war-weary townspeople found relaxation in the comparative peace of the countryside. The titles reissued in 1942 had a red-printed slip pasted to the half-title warning readers of changed conditions brought about by the war.

One of Sir Felix Pole's many contributions to the success of Great Western publicity was to bring in Miss Maxwell Fraser to write books and other publicity matter for the company. Maxwell Fraser, a Fellow of the Royal Geographical Society, and a very successful writer on the British countryside, was the daughter of W. H. Fraser the publicity agent. She was given the somewhat forbidding task of completely rewriting the descriptive sections of *Holiday Haunts*, and in addition wrote two sale publications, a slim volume on Southern Ireland published in 1932 and a major work on Somerset which appeared in 1934. Maxwell Fraser herself suggested that the GWR should publish a companion to the Mais books on Somerset, and K. W. C. Grand, then publicity agent, agreed to her writing a book of about 15,000 words on the county, with which she was very familiar. When the MS was completed it ran to 35,000 words! Grand read the MS during a journey on the 10.30 from Paddington and liked it so much that it was published in full.

Centenary year, 1935, saw the publication of W. Heath Robinson's *Railway Ribaldry*, a book of his inimitable cartoons dealing with many facets of Great Western history. This was, even by Great Western standards, very good value at a shilling a copy. Although this was the only new publication in 1935, the current stocks were selling steadily, and over 160,000 books were sold during the year.

The later 1930s saw little in the field of new books. W. G. Chapman's series for the railway enthusiasts, *The Cornish Riviera, Glorious Devon* and *Somerset*, and the rambling books, continued to sell steadily, and even the last reprint of *Abbeys*, first published back in 1925, was still in the book lists which appeared year by year in *Holiday Haunts* right up to the second war. In 1939 *Through the Window: Paddington to Penzance* was issued in a different format with half-tone illustrations, the only one of the series to be reissued. When war came again, and with it all the problems of paper rationing and labour shortage, and public preoccupation with more important matters than holidays, book publishing ceased. Manuscripts were already in hand for a new series of books on Somerset, Devon and Cornwall (the latter by Maxwell Fraser), but publication had to be abandoned.

At the end of the war, in 1945, the company published a slim quarto booklet *Dunkirk and the Great Western*, which told of the contribution of the GWR to the evacuation of the BEF from France. It heralded a brave attempt, but alas a short-lived one, to resume publishing after six years of inactivity. A series of small books of walks and motor tours for guests at Tregenna Castle and Manor House Hotels came out in 1946-7, and Christian Barman's *Next Station*, already mentioned, in the latter year. In 1947 too, the guide to Swindon works was revised and issued in a new format with more photographs, and put on general sale at 2s 6d (12½p). It proved to be one of the last books to be published by the company. It was later adapted and reissued in the same format, but without the roundel monogram on the cover, by British Railways, Western Region.

The printing, binding and warehousing of the publications was done through the stationery and printing department, who also despatched stocks to stations and offices, bookstalls and the book trade. Although the very low-priced booklets would not be an attractive proposition to a bookseller, the more important items in the Great Western list were stocked by bookshops and several attractive displays of the company's publications were shown in bookshop windows and were illustrated in the *Magazine* from time to time.

Lists of GWR publications were usually printed at the end of the books themselves, so that each title helped to sell the others, and every year several pages in *Holiday Haunts* were devoted to lists of books, jig-saw puzzles and other publicity matter. In the middle 30s a series of tiny folders, *The Literature of Locomotion*, were distributed free, and these contained full details of publications, including small reproductions of the book covers. Reviews of new titles appeared in the *Magazine*, as well, of course, as in the press and in railway periodicals. The many other means by which the company sold its books were too numerous to mention in detail. One of the earliest was an envelope, the back of which was closely printed with reviews of the early Broadley books. One of the most

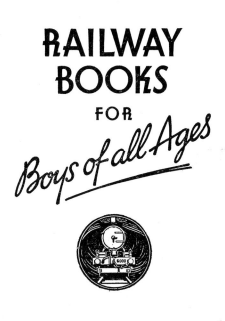

Illustrated folder advertising the *Boys of all Ages* series, c 1938 (actual size)

ingenious was a score-card for bowls, with an advertisement for *Holiday Haunts* on the reverse side, which was issued in the late 30s.

The Great Western was not, needless to say, the only railway to publish books. After the grouping the publicity departments of the other three big companies followed the lead given by Paddington twenty years earlier, but none of the other lines ever matched the Great Western in quantity or quality. Nevertheless, some of the rival companies' publications, particularly holiday guides, bore a strong resemblance to their Great Western prototypes. Imitation, it is said, is the sincerest form of flattery.

Chapter 5

Holiday Haunts

EARLY YEARS

'The object of this little volume is to impart to holiday-makers of all classes, noble and simple, rich and poor, strong and weak—such information as will enable them to secure a maximum of change, rest, pleasure or sport at a minimum of expenditure and fatigue.'

Thus ran the opening lines of the introduction to *Holiday Haunts on The Great Western Railway, Season 1906*. These words, and much else in the 334 pages of this first issue, are vivid reminders of the enormous gulf which divided the England of 1906 from the England of today.

Holiday Haunts made its appearance in the tranquil days of the pre-1914 era, when the Great Western was busy with new works aimed at shortening main lines and creating new through routes. 1906 was indeed a momentous year in the company's history—the year in which the 'Limited' first ran via Westbury, the year of the opening of the new harbour at Fishguard, and of the Cheltenham—Honeybourne line. These innovations brought with them the prospect of much extra holiday traffic, and in Edwardian England holiday traffic was a very important part of railway companies' income. The motor car, and still less the motor coach, had made little or no impression upon the railways' monopoly of transporting people from the towns to the country and seaside for their annual break.

It was therefore vitally important for the Great Western to publicise its new routes and improved services. As we have seen, a start had been made in 1904 with the publication of a book with the title *The Cornish Riviera,* and it was no coincidence that a few months later a new train was introduced, running non-stop from Paddington to Plymouth, to which James Inglis, the general manager, gave the same name.

Although holidays with pay for all were still far in the future, the holiday habit was increasing and the rise in the number of visitors to seaside resorts was creating a new industry—hotels, boarding houses and lodgings of a lesser kind proliferated, and the Great Western could render a valuable service both to the holidaymakers and to the seaside landladies by providing a comprehensive directory of the accommodation available in the resorts served by its trains.

The penny guide produced by Walter Hill, referred to in Chapter 1, had to some extent met this need, but with all the developments now taking place the authorities at Paddington were wise to take the guide under their own wing and develop it to the mutual advantage of the company, the passengers and the resorts.

It is not necessary to enumerate in detail all the changes in contents and style which were made in *Holiday Haunts* during its long life, but this first issue has so much of interest that it cannot be passed over without a brief look at its main features. It is not, perhaps, to the company's credit that the general arrangement of the book changed so little during most of the forty years of its existence.

The first issue had short introductory paragraphs about each county, with a few lines describing the main places of interest, arranged alphabetically. These were followed by a tabulated directory of accommodation, showing the distance from the nearest station and the facilities offered. The remarks column reminds us of the simple pleasures of Edwardian holidays and of the modest comforts then available in the lodgings and boarding-houses of the day. 'Facing sea', 'golf, fishing and bathing', 'good cooking and homely' were prominent, and there were some other attractions too—'bathroom and cycle room', 'pony and trap kept', 'stabling and rabbit shooting', while a farm in Gloucestershire offered 'attendance, bath and piano'. Accommodation was not graded by stars in those days, and intending guests had to select from the owners' descriptions: 'moderate', 'highly recommended', 'reasonable' or 'for medium class visitors'.

The directory was followed by further semi-displayed lists of hotels and boarding-houses, and the larger establishments had half or full-page displayed notices, set in the wide variety of fancy display type-faces then in vogue. Many of the advertisements included engravings, some of which were already distinctly old-fashioned, like that for the White Lion Royal Hotel, Bala, which was identical to one in use in guide books more than thirty years earlier. Distributed throughout the text were sections of art paper carrying half-tone reproductions of photographs, and a list of golf clubs and further displayed advertisements completed the volume.

There was a large folding map of the Great Western, showing the new Westbury and Badminton lines and also the GWR-GC joint line with the Great Western's own uncompleted Aynho section shown by dotted lines. There was also a separate map of the joint line to which the GWR was busy drawing attention as 'opening up rural districts for residential purposes'.

The Badminton line, then three years old, also had its share of attention, which included a photograph of the brand-new Badminton station, while the local Portcullis Hotel took a full-page advertisement with the headline Badminton—on the new main route to South Wales and the West—Two Hours from Paddington.

The new installations at Fishguard and the forthcoming opening of the 'short sea route *par excellence* to Ireland', also received due prominence, including advertisements for two of the company's hotels, the Hotel Wyncliffe at Goodwick (soon to be renamed The Fishguard Bay Hotel) and the South Wales Hotel at New Milford (Neyland) which it inherited from the old South Wales Railway.

As is to be expected, the largest sections were devoted to Devon and Cornwall, with emphasis on the advantages of Cornwall as a winter resort, and there were announcements of Special Monthly Season Tickets issued at Cornish stations. Passengers holding these tickets were allowed to take a Bicycle or Tricycle upon payment of 5s or 7s 6d (25p or 37½p).

The Westbury cut-off line also had a page to itself, headed

Page 107 (above) *Advertising motor car used in London early in 1907;* (below) *picture postcard from the first series, issued in 1904*

Page 108: *Jig-saw puzzle*, The Cheltenham Flyer, *issued 1933*

Important Announcement, and advising readers that the section between Langport and Castle Cary would open for through traffic on 1 July. Even this was not all, for yet another link in the modernisation chain came into use in 1906; this was the completion of two loops at Cheltenham and Chipping Norton Junction (Kingham) to allow through running from Gloucester and South Wales via the Banbury & Cheltenham Direct line to the Great Central. Another full page in the 1906 *Holiday Haunts* was devoted to these Cross Country Services which included Cardiff—Newcastle and also through workings from Birkenhead to Bournemouth and Dover 'without Change of Carriage'.

Yet among all these signs of the great awakening which had been planned before the turn of the century, and was now coming to fruition, were some curious anachronisms which are reminders of the fact that even in 1906 the horse was still in evidence, especially in rural districts. The White Lion Hotel at Barmouth still catered for 'posting in all its branches', the Emlyn Arms at Newcastle Emlyn announced that 'coaches for Cardigan start from door', and at St David's the City Hotel supplied post-horses and carriages. The motor car had its place, too, but in 1906 it was more an ally of the railway than the mortal enemy it was to become thirty years later. 'G.W.R. Motors and other Conveyances Daily' ran a line in the Whitsand Bay Hotel's advertisement, and the Gloucester Hotel at Weymouth claimed to be the only one in town with 'motor garage and inspection pit on the premises'.

From the outset, *Holiday Haunts* was one of the principal means of advertising the company's growing list of sale publications, and on page eight of the first issue the first of Broadley's books were listed as available 'from the Superintendent of the Line . . . on receipt of stamps'.

The price of the first issue of *Holiday Haunts* was one penny, and this remained the same for 1907, when the layout was similar except for a separate section of fifty pages on Southern Ireland, with its own map. The cover was also redesigned, both in the paper-bound edition and the cloth-bound version issued to hotels, clubs, enquiry offices and ships. With the 1908 issue the price was increased to threepence, fully justified by the increase in size

G

GREAT WESTERN RAILWAY.

Important ✿ ✿ ✿
✿ Announcement.

Shortening of the Route
to the West Country.

The section of line between **LANGPORT**
and **CASTLE CARY** will be opened for through
Express Traffic on

✿ ✿ JULY 1st. ✿ ✿

This is the latest enterprise in the direction
of providing a new direct Great Western route
to Somerset, Devon and Cornwall. The distance
saved, as compared with the existing route *via*
Bristol, is twenty miles, which will have the
effect of shortening the time occupied in the
journey from and to London, as well as adding
to the facilities afforded to passengers to and
from intermediate towns.

Announcement in the first issue of *Holiday Haunts*, 1906

to 588 pages, including the separate section for Southern Ireland and a new one for Brittany. The whole volume was printed on a cheap glazed paper and the separate art-paper plates were dispensed with. Archibald Edwards' slogan 'The Holiday Line' was used for the first time, and publications were well to the fore, including Broadley's books, now referred to as 'The Holiday Books of the Holiday Line', and picture post-cards (at a halfpenny each), while 'Fine Art Engravings', as used in carriages, were offered at a shilling each.

Road motors were much in evidence, with a photograph of a GWR charabanc, bulging with passengers, driving in solitary state down the centre of a deserted road in Cardiganshire, and frequent references in the text to this expanding branch of the company's services. There was also a full-page announcement of personally conducted sight-seeing tours of London by motor bus. A feature new in 1908 which remained until 1939 was a section of general information for travellers giving useful advice on luggage, tickets, timetables, reserved compartments and other matters, as well as information on publications, including the *Great Western Railway Magazine.*

Holiday Haunts' circulation was not confined to the British Isles. As early as 1909 some of the features were designed with an eye to overseas, particularly American, passengers. The Great Western Railway of England served many places which even then were great attractions for the Americans—Windsor, Stratford-upon-Avon and Bath among them.

'Breakfast, Luncheon and Dining Cars' (luncheon 2s 6d ($12\frac{1}{2}$p), five-course dinner 3s 6d ($17\frac{1}{2}$p)) were given due publicity, with photographs in 1908 and 1909 of the lush interiors of the 'Dreadnought' vehicles with their elaborately-carved walnut and morocco leather seats and decorative glass gangway door panels. The service, said the announcement, was 'unexcelled, with carefully prepared menus and gentlemanly attendants'.

The 1910 volume appeared, as usual, at Easter, and had a full-page notice of 'the new shortest route between London & Birmingham' (opened on 1 July), including a sketch-map showing the new line, and the old 'great way round' via Reading appeared unashamedly for comparison. As a frontispiece that year there was a photograph of engine No 4021 *King Edward*, of which 12 x 10in enlargements were offered at 2s 6d (12½p). In 1910, too, the plates were again printed on art paper, and this became a permanent feature.

In 1911 a new cover of white card was introduced, similar to those on Broadley's books, and this remained in use until 1928. The guide in its new guise was featured in a special double royal poster, of which 5,000 copies were printed and distributed throughout the system. At the same time the main folding map was placed in a pocket at the end of the English and Welsh section, and after 1911 the Brittany section was discontinued.

Holiday Haunts grew steadily in popularity throughout the pre-war years, and continued to appear annually until 1916, after which paper and labour restrictions prevented its publication until 1921. By the fourth issue (1909) the circulation had reached nearly 100,000 copies, and it remained at this figure until the war. In the *Jubilee of the Railway News* (1914) the Great Western's successful holiday guide was singled out for special praise by the author of the article on railway publicity—a Great Northern man.

In 1916 the printing dropped to 50,000 due to wartime conditions, and publication was resumed in May 1921 with an even smaller edition of 40,000. Meanwhile the size increased from 334 pages in 1906 to 620 pages in 1909. In 1911 and 1914 it ran to 668 pages, a size not exceeded for another ten years. The quality of the paper and of the plates improved, while the price had risen to sixpence by 1911 and remained at that very modest sum to the end, except for one or two first-war issues which reverted to threepence.

The descriptive text and historical matter in *Holiday Haunts* was the work of the ubiquitous A. M. Broadley, but for many years it was kept up to date by the staff of the publicity section working in conjunction with local authorities and through station masters. 'If any alteration or addition is desirable in the descriptive letterpress contained in the present Guide affecting any place served by your Station, please communicate with your Divisional Superintendent' ran an instruction of 1915. This was not all that these maids-of-all-work had to do in this connection. In the same

circular station masters were told that they must 'take steps forth-
with to secure renewals of advertisements in the present Guide,
and also to obtain new advertisements'. In this they were to be
helped by the company's advertising inspectors, and by the advertising agents, Messrs Wills Ltd. Station masters also had to collect
all the money received from advertisers—and all this in the midst
of traffic difficulties during a world war!

The actual printing of such a large volume, in which much of
the matter had to be hand composed in display types, was a major
task. The first issue was printed by Waterlow Bros and Layton;
there was a change to Wyman & Sons for the second issue and to
Butler & Tanner in 1909. Printing reverted to Wymans from 1912
to 1916. In addition to the complete volume, individual areas
were issued separately for a few years just prior to the 1914 war.

BETWEEN THE WARS

It might have been expected that the first post-war edition of
Holiday Haunts would have shown some major changes in
presentation and layout, but in fact the 1921 issue was a distinct
anti-climax. The general appearance was the same, the introduction was word for word as in 1916, except for the omission
of a few lines about Ireland, doubtless because of the political
situation there, and the book was reduced to 500 pages. One
redeeming feature was a new folding map by Emery Walker
which had a distinctly modern appearance and was the progenitor
of the GWR route map printed in red and black which, in various
forms, was in use for many years after the grouping. This 1921
guide was printed by William Brendon & Son Ltd of Plymouth,
the only issue produced by this firm.

Among the company's services given special prominence at this
time were the two-hour expresses on the Paddington to Birmingham route, the two-month tourist tickets, and the cross-country
services, and there were a number of full-page advertisements
with the aim of attracting industries to sites adjacent to the GWR,
with the caption 'Link Up With the Railway'.

Other main-line railway companies, naturally, had no place in
Holiday Haunts, but in 1922 there was a full-page advertisement

for the Festiniog and North Wales Narrow Gauge Railways, and the Snowdon Mountain Tramroad, and a photograph of a Fairlie locomotive and train at Tan-y-Bwlch. With the grouping already in the offing, the possibilities for increased holiday traffic were naturally being explored at Paddington, and the booklet *The Cambrian Coast*, ready before the end of 1922, was singled out for special mention in the introduction to the 1923 *Holiday Haunts*, where readers were reminded that 'the Great Western has become the Greater Great Western'.

Some of the earliest examples of the company's publicity set in Cheltenham type, to which allusion has already been made in Chapter 2, are to be found in the 1923 *Holiday Haunts*, including the new 'Go Great Western' slogan which on its first appearance in the previous year had been set in a popular face of the *art nouveau* era, De Vinne. A series of full-page announcements for Holiday Season Tickets in the 1924 issue was set entirely in Cheltenham type and for this reason bears some resemblance to handbills of the 1930s when this type was used in conjunction with the roundel monogram.

There were few changes in the physical make-up of the book in these early post-war years. In 1921 a separately-paged Special Supplement was added at the end, consisting of advertisements of shipping lines and a varied assortment of other firms (including, ironically, in 1921, one for 'The Real Holiday Spirit—B.P. Motor Spirit'), and from 1923 onwards there was a coloured frontispiece, which had been tried once before in 1911. The first real improvement came in 1924, when the printing of the plates was entrusted to a separate firm, Vandyck Printers Ltd, who specialised in gravure work. The gravure plates, printed in dark green and sepia, were a great improvement on the half-tones of earlier issues, and this beautiful process was used exclusively in future issues.

From 1922 until 1927 Wyman & Sons Ltd printed the text of *Holiday Haunts,* with the exception of the 1923 issue which was produced by Butler & Tanner, and the job reverted to the latter firm in 1928. They continued to print the text until the guide ceased publication with the 1947 issue. The pre-war practice of having a separate section for Southern Ireland was temporarily resumed for the years 1926-8, after which it was superseded by a separate publication.

Although W. H. Fraser had taken charge of the publicity department in 1924, his influence was not discernible in the appearance of *Holiday Haunts* for some time. It proceeded on its time-honoured way, with the opening paragraph of the introduction still much as it was in 1906; only in 1928 were the outdated references to 'noble and simple, rich and poor' omitted. But the circulation was increasing steadily, reaching 100,000 copies just after the grouping, 175,000 in 1926 and in 1928 no less than 200,000 copies were printed, a figure which was maintained until 1931, after which the depression made its impact on this, as on other publications.

It might be considered surprising that this publication, whose main features and physical appearance both dated back to the pre-1914 era, still sold so well. To the casual observer each issue looked much like the last, with only a change in colour of the GWR coat of arms and a new date on the cover, and there must have been many who assumed that the contents were likewise unchanged. The browsers round Wyman's bookstalls could hardly be expected to know that the publicity department staff (not to mention the station masters) were kept hard at work through a large part of the year bringing each issue up to date.

MODERNISATION

Changes, however, were soon to come. In 1928 the two travel books by S. P. B. Mais appeared, with their bold and attractive coloured covers, and at the same time the publicity department was preparing to provide the 1929 *Holiday Haunts* with covers of even brighter hues, with a red-costumed bathing beauty pictured against a vivid blue sky, and the words HOLIDAY HAUNTS standing out boldly in white. Even though the inside was the mixture as before, this and subsequent covers must have been largely responsible for the sales remaining around the 200,000 mark in 1929 and 1930 in spite of the onset of hard times.

The second major step forward came in the next issue, for which the descriptive text had been completely rewritten by

Maxwell Fraser, and the editor's name, for the first time, appeared on the title-page. Miss Fraser has given an excellent account in the *Magazine* of the work that went on both at Paddington and in the field to produce *Holiday Haunts*. She commenced work on the complete revision of the text in April 1929, travelling all over the Great Western system, personally visiting over 1,500 stations and halts to note down the special features and attractions of the innumerable places mentioned in the guide, and this task took her to the end of the year to complete. Thereafter one area was thoroughly revised each year, and minor amendments made in other areas.

The photographs, such an important feature of *Holiday Haunts*, were generally taken by the company's own photographers from the Engineering Department. The need to photograph engineering features, new buildings and works of all kinds took them to every part of the system, and they were therefore in a position to supply photographs of the scenic attractions of the line without incurring the expense of employing outside agents.

With a printing job as large as *Holiday Haunts* work had to start early. The contract for printing the gravure plates was let in July and by November the plates were printed and delivered in sheets to the firm responsible for the letterpress. The task of collecting the advertisements, through station masters and local agents, began in the summer and the complicated job of fitting all the thousands of advertisements, of various sizes, into the appropriate sections, occupied the publicity department staff until the end of November, when the completed copy had to be ready for the printers. Any odd spaces left on the advertisement pages were filled by inserting the company's own announcements. The stationery and printing department arranged the production of the necessary maps and the coloured cover and frontispiece, for which designs had been commissioned by the publicity department. By the end of the year all the separately printed components were at the main printers ready to be bound with the text.

Distribution of *Holiday Haunts* was the responsibility of the stationery department, who collected all the advance orders and instructed the printers to despatch parcels direct to stations, bookstalls, bookshops and other retail outlets. When all the copies

GREAT WESTERN RAILWAY

Season 1924

HOLIDAY HAUNTS

——IN——

ENGLAND, WALES

——AND——

CHANNEL ISLANDS

The Official Guide to the Holiday Resorts served by the G.W.R. with particulars of accommodation for holiday-makers and travellers generally.

PUBLISHED BY THE COMPANY
PADDINGTON STATION LONDON

GENERAL MANAGER • FELIX J. C. POLE

The title-page to *Holiday Haunts* which remained unaltered for twenty years until 1931 had been distributed and more were needed at specific places, stocks were transferred from points where sales were slower, and in this way the whole edition was usually disposed of.

The whole operation of the production demanded a high degree of co-operation between the publicity and stationery departments at Paddington, the editor, advertisers, station masters and the printers who produced the gravures, cover and text. Each year, from October to January, five members of the publicity staff moved to Frome, taking with them office equipment and machinery, so as to be close at hand while production at Butler & Tanner's works was under way. The enormous amount of paper required for 200,000 copies of a 1,000-odd page book was bought by separate contract and delivered in reels direct to the printer. Some 2,400 miles of paper, 36in wide, were used during *Holiday Haunts'* peak years.

The greatest circulation, achieved in the period 1928-31, was not maintained. In 1932 the number of copies actually sold fell to 123,675, and thereafter the printing order rose only slowly from 150,000 in 1933 to 172,000 in 1938. By far the greater number of copies were sold through the book trade. In 1931 the number sold at stations and offices was only 20,990, rising to 34,722 in 1938, about 20 per cent of the total. It is said that in its last years the income from advertisers, added to that received from the sale of the books, enabled the company to make a small profit on *Holiday Haunts*.

There were minor changes in layout during the remaining years. In 1931 the title-page, which had remained unaltered since before the first war, was slightly modified while retaining the classical motif, but for the centenary issue in 1935 it was completely modernised and incorporated a speeding 'King' and the roundel. The 1931 issue was greatly improved by division into areas instead of counties and by the insertion of attractive gravure sub-titles to each section. In 1933 the gravure illustrations were completely restyled, with larger blocks and inset captions in sans-serif type. Many of the plates were full-page, and apart from the title-page, which was now quite out of keeping with the rest, *Holiday Haunts* had, by this year, assumed a really modern look. The next year's issue was the largest ever produced, running to 1,054 pages.

HOLIDAY HAUNTS

SEASON 1935

G.W.R. CENTENARY NUMBER

The G.W.R. Official Guide
to Holiday Resorts in

ENGLAND, WALES CHANNEL ISLANDS AND ISLE OF MAN

By MAXWELL FRASER, F.R.G.S.

• • •

With particulars of
accommodation for
holiday-makers and
travellers generally.

• • •

PUBLISHED BY THE COMPANY
PADDINGTON STATION, LONDON

General Manager
JAMES MILNE

March, 1935.

Title-page to the centenary issue of *Holiday Haunts*, 1935

The centenary of the company was celebrated with a bold cover in chocolate, cream and gold, and an inset sixteen page coloured supplement which did scant justice to the occasion and whose design was in the worst possible taste. In 1932 Eric Gill's sans-serif type had begun to appear in the company's advertisements in the guide, and by 1935 had almost, but not entirely, supplanted Cheltenham for this purpose. Among these advertisements were pages devoted to W. G. Chapman's new book *Cheltenham Flyer*, the ever-popular jig-saw puzzles, the two books by Mais and Maxwell Fraser's *Somerset*. On the traffic side, the Land Cruises were well to the fore, and in 1935 there was a full-page advertisement for the Railway Air Services. The Great Western had introduced their pioneer flights back in 1931, but for some reason they were never mentioned in *Holiday Haunts* until four years later. In 1935, too, two pages were devoted to the Door-to-Door Containers for household removals and for general goods traffic.

THE LAST YEARS

After the centenary, production of *Holiday Haunts* continued in much the same style, but with increasing competition from the motor car and motor coach and also, let it be said, from similar publications now being issued by the other group companies, the sales figures never reached the 1931 peak and the size of the guide declined steadily from 1,032 pages in 1937 to 744 pages in 1940. *Holiday Haunts* was no longer the unique publication it had been in earlier days. The trends in holidaymaking, and the desperate efforts made by the GWR to keep its summer passenger traffic were everywhere apparent in the pages of its holiday guide. Camping coaches had a page from 1936, the new Travel Savings Cards from 1938, and in that year four pages were devoted to Holiday Season Tickets.

The coronation in 1937 was marked by a vivid red, white and blue cover depicting children (one of them holding a Union Jack) around a sand castle bearing the crown and royal cipher picked out in pebbles.

When the war came in September 1939 the next year's issue was, of course, well in hand, and in spite of the inevitable dislocation, it duly appeared in the fateful spring of 1940, with 744 pages and a 'utility' cover with a plain half-tone illustration. For six years *Holiday Haunts*, like most other publications of its kind, ceased to make its customary appearance on the bookstalls at Easter, but in December 1944, with the war still in progress, the government agreed to release Maxwell Fraser, who was then on the staff of the *Slough Observer*, so that she could return to the Great Western to commence the task of once more revising the descriptive text of *Holiday Haunts*. This she did with her accustomed thoroughness, taking special care over the areas devastated by wartime bombing. In the spring of 1947, with the war over but the shadow of nationalisation already deepening over the railways, the thirty-second and last edition of the guide, once more resplendent in a coloured cover, was issued from Paddington. Printed by Butler & Tanner, with gravure plates by the Sun Engraving Co Ltd, it contained 688 pages. The price, notwithstanding increases in cost, was still held at the traditional sixpence ($2\frac{1}{2}$p).

The long and placid life of *Holiday Haunts*, extending over a period of almost forty years, spanning two world wars, is only one illustration of the unique character of the Great Western Railway. In its early years ultra-conservative, it nevertheless did its job well, and gained the respect both of its readers and of its numerous advertisers. The guide never lost its individuality, and like those bygone, but immortal slogans which it helped to propagate—'The Cornish Riviera', 'The Holiday Line' and 'Go Great Western', its very title has found a permanent place in the vocabulary, as well as in the hearts, of travellers in 'The Western Land'.

Chapter 6

Miscellaneous Forms of Publicity

LANTERN LECTURES AND FILMS

In common with many other organisations and commercial firms, the Great Western Railway issued series of lantern slides which could be borrowed by clubs, societies and individuals. They first appeared in the General Information pages of *Holiday Haunts* in 1914, when fifteen series, complete with lecture notes, were available. These ranged from a short lecture with twenty-nine slides on Shakespeare's Country to one of 105 slides describing a journey from Cheshire to the West Country.

No charge was made for borrowing, and carriage was free inside GWR delivery areas. The demand was considerable: in the early 1930s up to 1,500 applications for slides were received in the winter season. There were at that time over a hundred sets, containing in all some 8,000 slides. In the 1920s and 30s the lectures were revised and new series were added, while from about 1934 the lecture notes appeared with redesigned covers carrying a large roundel monogram.

Although the popularity of lantern lectures had declined by the outbreak of the second war, they were still in demand for educational purposes and as late as 1946 a few of the lectures were reissued, the new edition of the notes having coloured covers and text set in Gill Sans type in the style then being adopted by the company. This style, suitably adapted, was used when the remainder of the lecture notes were reissued by British Railways Western Region shortly after nationalisation.

Just before the second war it had been the intention of the

Check list of Lantern Lectures, see page 185

Two lantern lecture booklets, c 1934 and 1947. The one on Oxford, with cream lettering in Gill Sans, on a brown background, shows the style adopted in the short post-war period

publicity department to supplement, and largely replace, the lantern lectures by cinematograph films, but the war put a stop to this enterprise after only one production, *Cornwall, the Western Land*. This film, however, was not by any means the first to be produced by the company. In the *Magazine* for October 1904 it was stated that 'arrangements have recently been made with the Biograph Company to take a series of animated pictures of the North Wales districts . . . which are being exhibited at the Empire Theatre, London'. It would seem likely that this was the first Great Western film, and it is not entirely surprising that it was made during the short period of two years which also saw the publication of the pioneer book *The Cornish Riviera* and the first issue of *Holiday Haunts*.

By 1912 several more films had been made, including one on Devon and Cornwall and one showing scenes in the Wye Valley. These were shown at 'a successful Cinematograph Exhibition' at the Northern Polytechnic in the spring of that year, and attracted an audience of about 1,000, 'many of whom, we hope, will visit Devon and Cornwall during the coming holiday season'. The making of these films is described in some detail in the *Magazine* for November 1912. Two films were made in Cornwall, one of which was in a crude colour process known as Kinemacolour. The company supplied transport for the film unit, and some of the filming was done from road motors and from a goods brake van hauled by an 0–6–0 saddle tank engine. Shots were also taken at Paddington, in a dining car, at Plymouth and on Saltash bridge.

Two years later on 20 May 1914 the company arranged its own Cinematograph Matinee at the London Coliseum. The programme, which covered most parts of the Great Western system, was entitled 'The Story of the Holiday Line told by Living Pictures', and a 28-page illustrated booklet was issued to the 'large and distinguished audience'. Holiday travel was again the theme, but there were shots of a train leaving Paddington, of Swindon works, of an engine taking water at speed, and of RMS *Mauretania* arriving at Fishguard. The *Magazine* mentions that 'during the display musical selections were given . . . and appropriate songs rendered', and that the films were 'received with much interest and enthusiasm'.

JIG-SAW PUZZLE

Size of Puzzle, 20" x 12".

ABOUT 150 PIECES

ABOUT 150 PIECES

"SPEED."

Manufactured by The Chad Valley Co., Ltd., Harborne, England.

Published by The Great Western Railway Company.

ABOUT **200** PIECES INTERLOCKING – THREE PLY WOOD

JIG-SAW

GWR

PUZZLE

PUBLISHED BY THE GREAT WESTERN RAILWAY CO.
MANUFACTURED BY THE CHAD VALLEY CO LTD. HARBORNE, ENGLAND.

Page 125 (above) *Earlier pattern of jig-saw puzzle box;* (left) *later type of book box*

HALL GREEN.

THE district around Hall Green, the first station on the North Warwickshire Line after passing the Junction at Tyseley, and only 5 miles from Birmingham, is growing rapidly in public estimation as a residential centre. Bracing air, well wooded in parts and in others open, it offers many ideal excursions to the pedestrian. For those preferring the 9-hole course of the Hall Green Golf Club (situated about 10 minutes' walk from the station), and, for the angler, the River Cole and Trittiford Mill Pool provide excellent sport. A bowling green is under construction.

Several building estates are being developed, and ample land is available for those desirous of building their own houses.

FARES TO BIRMINGHAM.

Ordinary Fares.

	First.	Third.
	s. d.	s. d.
Single	0 9	0 5
Return	1 3	0 6

Season Ticket Rates.

	First.	Third.
	£ s. d.	£ s. d.
1 Month	0 15 0	0 7 6
3 ,,	2 1 0	1 0 0
12 ,,	8 2 6	4 0 0

Population, 2,500.

Early Closing, Wednesday.

Altitude, 460 ft. above sea level.

Subsoil, Sand and Marl.

Local Authority, City of Birmingham.

Recreation, Golf, Tennis, Fishing, Cricket, Gymnasium.

Rail distance from Birmingham, 5 miles.

Time occupied, 14 minutes.

Train Service, 25 trains to and 27 from Birmingham.

Rents, from £29 per annum.

Rates, 6s. 6d. in the £.

Gas, 3s. 11d. per 1,000 cubic ft.

Water, 1s. 6d. in the £.

YARDLEY WOOD.

YARDLEY WOOD, another village in the heart of healthy bracing country served by the North Warwickshire Line, will in the near future be a popular residential neighbourhood owing to its close proximity to Birmingham, and its picturesque surroundings. The 9-hole course of the Robin Hood Golf Club can be reached in half an hour. Fishing at a small charge is obtainable in the Trittiford Mill Pool, and boating may be enjoyed on the G.W.R. Canal, close to the station.

Land is available for building.

FARES TO BIRMINGHAM.

Ordinary Fares.

	First.	Third.
	s. d.	s. d.
Single	0 9	0 5
Return	1 6	0 9

Season Ticket Rates.

	First.	Third.
	£ s. d.	£ s. d.
1 Month	0 16 6	0 8 6
3 ,,	2 5 0	1 2 6
12 ,,	...	...

Population, 3,000.

Early Closing, Wednesday.

Altitude, 450 ft. above sea level.

Subsoil, Sand and Gravel.

Local Authority, City of Birmingham.

Recreation, Fishing and Boating, Golf.

Rail distance from Birmingham, 6 miles.

Time occupied, 18 minutes.

Train Service, 23 trains per day each way.

Rents, about £29 per annum.

Rates, 7s. 6d. in the £.

Gas, 1s. 11d. per 1,000 cubic ft.

Water, without 6/3 or £30 property.

1.—HALL GREEN—SOUTHAM ROAD.

2.—YARDLEY WOOD STATION.

19

BUSINESS MAN'S TIME TABLE.

Section II.—PERSHORE, EVESHAM, STRATFORD-ON-AVON and BIRMINGHAM.

Week-days.

Up Trains.

The Service is given of trains arriving at Birmingham before 12 no.on. For complete time table see Official Time Book.

		a.m. Via Worcester.	a.m.	a.m. Via Worcester.	a.m. M	a.m. Via Worcester.
Pershore	dep.	7 38	...	...	...	...
Flodbury	...	7 44	...	...	...	...
Evesham	...	7 53	...	8 48	9 13	9 16
Littleton and Badsey	...	7 57	...	8 45	9 32	9 16
Honeybourne	{ arr. dep. }	...	...	8 34 8 45	9 39 9 5	9 16
Broad Marston Halt	...	8 15	...	9 1	10 9	...
Long Marston	...	8 29	...	9 6	10 16	...
Milcote	...	...	...	...	10 16	...
Chambers Crossing Halt	...	...	...	...	10 24	...
Evesham Road Crossing Halt	...	...	...	9 13	10 26	...
Stratford-on-Avon	arr.	8 57	...	9 20	...	...
BIRMINGHAM (Snow Hill)	arr.	9 22	10 5	10* 0	11 26 11 36	...

M Rail Motor Car, One Class only.   * Birmingham (Moor Street) Station.

Section II.—BIRMINGHAM, STRATFORD-ON-AVON, EVESHAM and PERSHORE.

Week-days.

Down Trains.

The Service is given of trains leaving Birmingham after 3.0 p.m. For complete time table see Official Time Book.

		p.m.	p.m. Via Worcester.	p.m.	p.m. Via Worcester.	p.m. M	p.m.	p.m. Via Worcester.	p.m. Weds. & Sats. exep. Via Worcester.	p.m. Weds. & Sats. only.
BIRMINGHAM (Snow Hill)	dep.	3 55	3 55	4 45	4 45	...	5 55	6 30	8 30	8 * 20
Stratford-on-Avon	{ arr. dep. }	4 29 4 31	...	5 12 5 12	...	...	6 47	...	...	...
Evesham Road Crossing Halt	...	...	...	5 15	...	...	...	...	...	...
Chambers Crossing Halt	...	...	...	5 17	...	...	...	...	...	...
Milcote	...	4 47	...	5 33	...	...	6 53	8 36	...	...
Long Marston	...	4 53	...	5 49	...	...	6 59	8 42	...	...
Broad Marston Halt	...	...	...	...	...	...	...	...	...	...
Honeybourne	{ arr. dep. }	5 5 5 26	...	6 2 ...	...	...	7 9 7 29	8 49 8 57	10 38 11 43	11 19 11 47
Littleton and Badsey	...	5 33	...	...	...	...	7 36	...	...	...
Evesham	...	5 43	6 5	...	...	...	7 35	9 24	10 50 11 41	...
Flodbury	...	5 50	...	...	...	...	...	...	...	...
Pershore	...	5 55	...	...	...	...	...	...	...	...

M Rail Motor Car, One Class only.

Section II.—BIRMINGHAM, GREAT ALNE and ALCESTER.

Week-days.

		a.m.	a.m.	p.m.	p.m.
Birmingham (Snow Hill)	dep.	8 20	9 33	4 8	5 10
Great Alne	...	8 37	9 40	5 10	7 3
Alcester	arr.	9 22	10 34	5 17	7 10

Week-days.

		a.m.	a.m.	p.m.	p.m.
Alcester	dep.	8 20	...	4 8	8 10
Great Alne	arr.	8 27	9 43	5 10	...
Birmingham (Snow Hill)	arr.	9 22	10 34	5 17	7 10

N.B.—These time tables are subject to alteration.

18

In addition to these films produced as part of the company's publicity, the Great Western played an important part in the making of a number of commercial films which had a railway setting. In the early days of the 'talkies' Conan Doyle's *The Hound of the Baskervilles* was filmed by Gainsborough Pictures Ltd on the Moretonhampstead branch and at the GWR Manor House Hotel, and in the same year, 1931, perhaps the best-known of these films, *The Ghost Train*, was shot at Camerton, near Bath, and on Barmouth bridge.

The showing of *The Ghost Train* gave the Great Western an ideal opportunity to exploit its publicity value, and elaborate 'station' scenes were provided in the foyers of cinemas, together with posters, and a special folder *See the Ghost Train Country* was distributed to audiences. A fully illustrated account of the making of this famous film is given in the *Magazine* for August 1931.

The Great Western always met the requests of film companies for assistance in adding realism to railway scenes, and often went to great trouble to provide stock, staff, equipment and even special trains. Even in centenary year, when there was more than enough extra work, Twickenham Studios were provided with several special trains, enough engine parts to make a complete cab mock-up, facilities for cameramen at Paddington and points on the line, and partial occupation of the Basingstoke branch on two Sundays. The result was an hour-long thriller *The Last Journey*, which included some highly dubious operating and a collision averted at the last moment. From this unlikely situation the Great Western nevertheless received some good publicity in the film's foreword in which the company's help was acknowledged. It concluded with these words:

Apart from the interest which the portrayal of a great railway system must arouse, it is, perhaps, amusing to reflect that, actually, the Great Western would be the very last railway on which the events pictured in the film could actually happen, as it has become a recognised truism with the travelling public that the Great Western Railway is not only the fastest and most comfortable, but also the safest railway system in the British Empire.

H

Later in 1931 the Gaumont British Picture Corporation was given facilities to take sound recordings at Paddington and on various express trains, for use in the film *The Rome Express*—with some lack of authenticity! The first official sound films were made in 1933, consisting of three travel films with the titles *Dawdling in Devon*, *By Cornish Coasts*, and *Wandering by the Wye*. These were on general release in the provinces and copies were also sent to the United States.

Two years later the occasion of the Great Western company's centenary offered a unique opportunity for the making of a film on the history of the line. Under the direction of Walter Creighton, Merton Park Studios produced the centenary film *The Romance of a Railway* in close collaboration with the company. The replica of *North Star* and a period train were provided, and many of the parts were played by members of the GWR London and Swindon Operatic Societies. Shots depicting the formation of the company in 1833 were taken in the Merchants' Hall in Bristol, while among the studio scenes was one showing a reconstruction of Brunel's office. The historical part of the film was followed by scenes on the GWR system and shots of Swindon works and various traffic operations.

The film was shown at the centenary celebrations at Bristol and at the London banquet, and was later put on in various parts of the system so that the staff could have an opportunity of seeing it. At each showing a senior officer of the company spoke to the audience on their part in maintaining the long tradition of the Great Western. Fortunately the centenary film has survived, and while it is not in the first class by modern standards, it is nevertheless an historic and precious relic of the Great Western.

In the following year, 1936, Strand Films made *Duchy of Cornwall* for the company, and in 1939 *Great Western Railway Approaches* was produced by G-B Instructional Films.

By this time the magic had gone from the magic lantern show, and a series of 16mm sound and silent films was planned, to replace the lantern slides. The first of these, *Cornwall—The Western Land*, appeared in 1939, with a fine opening shot of a 'Castle' class engine *Isambard Kingdom Brunel* hauling 'The Bristolian' near Chippenham. This was to have been used for the titles of the whole series, but owing to the outbreak of war no further films were made. As the company had clearly realised the value of films, both for cinema audiences and for loan to smaller groups, it is likely that but for the war some films of real railway interest would have been produced, perhaps on the lines of W. G. Chapman's highly successful books, and their value to the railway enthusiast of today would have been inestimable.

At least one film appeared during the second world war— *Christmas Travel*, which was made in 1941, and in 1947 the increasing concern with publicity for goods services was reflected in the issue of a film with the title *Freight*, which was shown on the GWR stand at various exhibitions. In this last year of the independent railways the four main-line companies collaborated in the production of a film *Pathways to Perfection, or Four Famous Trains,* in which the Great Western contribution was, needless to say, the 'Cornish Riviera Express'.

EXHIBITIONS

Although the Society of Arts had held a small exhibition of machinery and models as early as 1761, the Great Exhibition, held in the Crystal Palace in Hyde Park ninety years later, was the first occasion on which a comprehensive range of the products of the world's industries had been on view to the public.

The railways, besides providing a public service, were also manufacturers on a large scale, and in the great exhibitions of the Victorian era their exhibits were primarily, if not entirely, aimed at showing the locomotives, rolling stock and equipment made in their own workshops. In more recent times much of the novelty of the steam engine and of railways generally has gone, and railway companies' stands at exhibitions tended more and more to depict with photographs, maps and other graphic means, the services they had to offer rather than the equipment used in providing them.

When the Great Exhibition opened on 1 May 1851 the 'Gauge War' on the railways was still raging and the fine engines designed by Daniel Gooch and built at Swindon were keeping the broad gauge Great Western well ahead of its narrow-gauge rivals in speed. The *Great Western* of 1846 paved the way for the 4–2–2 'Iron Duke' class which began to appear in 1847. Of these great 8-foot singles the most famous, *Lord of the Isles*, built in March 1851, was exhibited by the company at the Crystal Palace, where the conditions were ideal for comparing her magnificent proportions with the much smaller narrow-gauge engines of the day. The engine was awarded a bronze medal which was afterwards presented by the directors to Daniel Gooch.

The company did not exhibit at the International Exhibition at South Kensington in 1862, but *Lord of the Isles,* by that time withdrawn from service and preserved, alas, only temporarily, at Swindon, was again shown at the Edinburgh Exhibition in 1890. Three years later the Great Western went to considerable trouble and expense in connection with the World's Columbian Exhibition at Chicago. The centrepiece was again *Lord of the Isles*, but in addition there was a large collection of photographs of rolling stock and scenes on the line, a sectional drawing of the Severn Tunnel, a complete vacuum brake assembly, cut away to show the working parts, and a panel displaying various sections of rail. The exhibits were despatched from Swindon by the White Star liner *Tauric*, which had a singularly rough voyage, described in some detail by B. J. Hall, a Swindon man who was in charge of the exhibits, in the *Magazine*.

No doubt at this time, and later, there were other, smaller exhibitions to which the Great Western contributed, but which have gone unchronicled. One which did get a mention in the *Magazine*, largely because it was held in connection with the GWR Temperance Union, was a small exhibition at Exeter in November 1895, when the company showed models and photographs. One of the other attractions was a 'fine collection of paintings' by F. Moore, whose coloured post-cards are so much sought after today.

At the Scottish National Exhibition at Glasgow in 1911 the company's stand included a large model of the turbine steamer *St George* used on the Fishguard—Rosslare service. Later in that year a much more ambitious display was mounted at the Coronation Exhibition at the White City, where a large collection of photographs of rolling stock, old timetables, posters and models of

The Great Bear and the steamer *St Patrick* were displayed on a stand decked with flags and large banners bearing the motto 'G.W.R. The Holiday Line'. A headboard running the length of the stand proclaimed the Great Western as 'The Line of 1,000 Stations', while in the centre of the stand was a stall where tickets, books and post-cards were on sale.

The Shakespeare's England Exhibition at Earl's Court in the following year provided a marked contrast to most events of the kind. Here the GWR had an office in an impressive and realistic half-timber building with small mullioned windows, leaded lights, and overhanging upper storeys. A fine hanging sign bearing the company's arms within a garter and the words GREAT WESTERN RAILWAY completed this Tudor scene. Inside were large photographs of scenery on the line, illuminated in colour.

At this time the fittings and display stands were themselves examples of the best craftsmanship, in contrast to the hardboard and plywood of the modern exhibitions. When war broke out in August 1914 the company had a stand at the Anglo-American Exhibition at the White City, and a description in the *Magazine* mentions three mahogany counters and a 'handsome canopy supported on eight mahogany columns, with eight finely carved head boards . . .' The canopy was draped with pink and white 'relieved by plush hangings'. Lighting was provided by two 'ornamental electroliers shaped like water lilies'.

Without doubt the largest and most interesting display mounted by the GWR at a public exhibition was at the British Empire Exhibition held at Wembley in 1924-5. The exhibition itself was the biggest ever staged in this country, and no less than 27 million people visited it. In the Palace of Engineering the recently built *Caerphilly Castle* was on show from May to October 1924, and during the same period in 1925 her place was taken by *Pendennis Castle,* fresh from her exchange trials with the LNER 'Pacifics', one of which, *Flying Scotsman,* was placed next to the Great Western engine. This is not the place to discuss the controversy which raged over these trials, but the enormous interest shown by the public and by railway enthusiasts in Collett's engines is clearly indicated not only by the three-quarters of a million people who mounted the footplates, but also by the demand for Chapman's book

Caerphilly Castle and the jig-saw puzzle of the engine, both of which were on sale at the GWR kiosk at Wembley.

In addition to the locomotives claimed by Swindon to be the most powerful passenger locomotives in the British Isles, the Great Western exhibit included a complete signal box, manned by signalmen who demonstrated the working. A small brochure was issued free to visitors to the box. Models of Newport, Cardiff and Barry docks were also shown, and there were the usual photographs and maps. A rather uninspiring souvenir booklet was issued, containing some coloured and sepia illustrations and a map of the system.

The second season of the Exhibition coincided with the Railway Centenary, and a special section was devised at Wembley in 1925 to mark the event. The Great Western exhibit, in addition to *Pendennis Castle*, included the Dynamometer Car, a 20-ton wagon, Queen Victoria's coach of 1850, the replica *North Star* and a number of smaller items. The original *North Star* having been cut up early in 1906, together with *Lord of the Isles*, the Swindon authorities did their best to expiate their sins by building a replica, utilising the few surviving parts of the original engine. This was built as the company's principal contribution to the Stockton & Darlington Centenary exhibition which was held from 1 to 18 July, after which *North Star* was moved to Wembley.

The souvenir booklet for 1925 was an improvement on the 1924 issue, and gave details of the GWR exhibits as well as a survey of the services and facilities offered by the company. Quite apart from the Great Western's exhibits at Wembley, the Exhibition brought considerable extra passenger revenue to the company, involving nearly 800 special trains which carried over 384,000 passengers.

The publicity department, and indeed most other sections of the company's organisation, were certainly kept busy in 1925 with these two major events. For the procession of locomotives and rolling stock which ran from Stockton to Darlington on 2 July 1925 the Great Western sent, in addition to *North Star*, four locomotives which were in normal service; 4082 *Windsor Castle*, heading the GWR Royal Train, No 111 *Viscount Churchill* (the rebuilt *Great Bear*—a rather odd choice), drawing a train of articulated stock, Churchward's splendid mixed-traffic 2–8–0 No 4700, and a 2–8–0 tank engine No 5225.

At Wembley there was one other event of 1925 in which the Great Western had a part. The referee of the Cup Final that year was Capt W. E. Russell, a clerk at Swindon works.

Great as was the publicity value of the 'Castles' at Wembley in 1924-5, the Great Western gained even more prestige from an event in 1927, when the first of the new 'Kings', No 6000 *King George V,* completed in June of that year, was shipped to America to take part in the centenary of Baltimore & Ohio Railroad.

The appearance of *King George V* at Baltimore was the outcome of a request from the organiser of the centenary exhibition to Sir Felix Pole, who agreed to send the new engine, and also the *North Star* replica, on condition that the Great Western should be the sole representative of the British railways. The entire cost of shipment and maintenance while in America was borne by the Baltimore & Ohio. With the engines went W. A. (later Sir William) Stanier, Driver W. Young and Fireman G. Pearce, and two Swindon fitters.

The visit was a triumph; the clean lines and superb finish of the 'King', in marked contrast to the untidy appearance of American engines, created a great impression both on the public and on railway officials. As railways originated in England, *King George V* was given pride of place at the head of the daily procession of engines, and after the exhibition she drew a special train, including a dynamometer car, from Baltimore to Washington and Philadelphia, and back to Baltimore, when, in spite of poor coal and an unfamiliar road, she acquitted herself well. She returned to England with the brass bell and centenary medals which have adorned this historic locomotive ever since.

Between the wars the number and variety of exhibitions increased considerably. Many of these, like the British Industries Fair, the Motor Show, the Ideal Home Exhibition and the Schoolboys' Exhibition, became annual events. Railway exhibits were not appropriate to many of the events, but the larger exhibitions brought considerable extra passenger traffic and many excursions were run from the provinces to London, while enquiry offices were usually provided by individual companies or jointly by the four main-line companies.

One of the earliest combined publicity schemes by the four companies after the grouping was an elaborate stand at the Advertising Exhibition held at Olympia in July 1927, in which the principal aim was to convince industry and traders of the cheapness of rail freight transport. On a lighter note, the Great Western had its own stand at the Health and Hygiene Exhibition at Manchester in 1929. Here that great stand-by, the Cornish Riviera, was the theme, with an artificial beach complete with sand, shells and seaweed, a pierrot troupe, the Railway Queen (who partook of tea under a canopy on the sands) and rides on a real live donkey. Strategically placed, of course, was a stall well laden with *Holiday Haunts*, of which nearly 1,500 copies were sold.

Another railway centenary, that of the Liverpool & Manchester Railway, occurred in 1930, and at the exhibition in St George's Hall, Liverpool, the Great Western showed models, including one of the 9.10 p.m. Paddington—Birkenhead goods train, and sold books and jig-saw puzzles from a kiosk. At Wavertree station the replica *North Star* was once again on view, and the brand new *King Stephen* was also shown.

In the 1930s the need to reduce expenditure, and the gradual closing of the ranks of the railway companies in the face of increasing competition from the road, could both be seen in publicity policy. To an increasing extent the four main-line companies collaborated by having joint stands at exhibitions. At the Schoolboys' Exhibition of 1931 a combined exhibit, including GWR signal apparatus, was supplied, with a headboard bearing the prophetic slogan 'British Railways', and in the years up to the outbreak of the second war joint stands were provided at the Ideal Home Exhibition, at the 1935 Brussels Exposition, at the South African Exhibition in Johannesburg in 1936, and at the Empire Exhibition at Glasgow in 1938.

The scope for economy in this form of publicity can be judged from the fact that in 1937 there were no less than thirteen exhibitions at Olympia and the Royal Agricultural Hall alone, where the GWR was represented individually or jointly. Exhibitions were multiplying abroad too. At the Canadian National Exhibition at

Toronto in 1938 a model of a Great Western diesel rail-car was on view at the joint stand of the British companies, and the GWR collaborated in a joint British exhibit at the New York World's Fair in 1939, at which the principal attraction was the LMS 'Coronation Scot' train.

In the short post-war period between the end of hostilities and nationalisation, the only exhibitions of importance to which the company contributed were nevertheless very appropriate settings for Great Western publicity. The first was the Welsh Industries Fair which opened at the Royal Agricultural Hall on New Year's Day 1947. In spite of the shortage of materials which hampered so much activity at that time, the GWR stand was a very attractive and well-designed example of modern display technique. Large photographs of ships, trains and docks, the familiar model of *King George V* from the Lawn at Paddington, and a model of one of the new Channel Islands steamers then nearing completion were on view, and there was a continuous showing of films, including *Freight* and one on Cardiff docks, of which there was also a model. As a foretaste of things to come, some of the seats then being installed in new restaurant cars were on show.

The second exhibition of that year—and the last—was the Industrial Wales exhibition at Olympia in August and September. Here the GWR and LMS had a joint stand, a modest but effective display with a huge map of Wales, showing the railways, and incorporating the two companies' monograms—and a panel of photographs of various railway features in the Principality.

ADVERTISING ROAD MOTOR CARS

There is a strange irony in the fact that the Great Western Railway used some of its road motor cars to keep the public informed about railway services. In 1905, less than three years after the inauguration of the first motor bus service between Helston and the Lizard, a bus was equipped with bill boards and put on the road to advertise GWR Christmas services and to publicise the Cornish Riviera as a winter resort. In the following year the *Magazine* reported with obvious pride that 'up to December 7 the Company's Advertising Car in Scotland had run a distance of 1,665 miles over roads of all descriptions without any mechanical failure'.

Again, in 1908, a standard GWR 30hp Milnes-Daimler bus was driven from Slough to Carlisle in three days and toured Scotland without trouble in the depth of winter. It seems that Great Western road motors were as well maintained as their locomotives. In 1910 another bus toured the north of England, and there were extended tours of the midlands and north in 1913-14. In addition to displaying posters, the buses carried a stock of publications and free travel literature, and an advertising inspector accompanied the vehicles.

Road traffic in those days was very light, and the buses could move slowly through populated areas without causing the chaos which would result from such a practice today. The impact, particularly in smaller and more remote places, must have been considerable, and the Great Western advertising motor cars were certainly one of the most enterprising, as well as the most novel, forms of publicity ever adopted by the company.

The 1914-18 war put a stop to these tours, but by 1922 buses were back on the road and one toured seventy towns in the north in June and July of that year, visiting factories, clubs and institutes. Even though it was summertime, it must have been an exhausting trip for the crew; the AEC double-deck bus had solid tyres and an open cab. In 1928 much more comfortable vehicles, two Thornycroft single-deckers, with enclosed cabs and pneumatic tyres, made what seems to have been the last of these tours, again in the north of England and Scotland.

JIG-SAW PUZZLES

To anyone whose childhood embraced the inter-war years, the most familiar form of Great Western publicity, though perhaps not recognised as such, was the series of jig-saw puzzles produced for the company by a well-known firm of toy and game manufacturers, The Chad Valley Co Ltd, of Harborne, Birmingham.

Apart from the travel books, the jig-saw puzzles were undoubtedly the most successful venture in what Sir Felix Pole called propaganda, that the company ever entered on. For their origin we have to go back to the British Empire Exhibition, held at Wembley in 1924-5. The 4-6-0 engine No 4073 Caerphilly Castle was displayed by the GWR on its stand in the Palace of Engineering, and it was a happy thought to have available on the stand a replica of this new and handsome engine, in a form which would delight the thousands of youngsters who crowded the exhibition.

This, the first of a series which ran to no less than forty-four different puzzles, bore a side view of the engine, from a photograph, printed in three colours, and measured 29 x 9in. The puzzle comprised 150 pieces, made of good-quality plywood and packed in an attractive box. The price when it appeared in May 1924 was five shillings (25p), but a month later this was reduced to 2s 6d (12½p), which was about a third of the cost of comparable puzzles published elsewhere. It was first sold at Wembley but soon appeared on the bookstalls and was, of course, also available from Paddington.

Consideration was given to producing the puzzle in cardboard at an even lower price, but the company wisely decided, in true Great Western tradition, to put quality above other considerations, and the entire series was produced in plywood.

Caerphilly Castle, appropriately, got off to a flying start. Soon letters were coming in to Paddington from people who claimed to have completed the puzzle in record time—one man who wrote in August 1924 had accomplished it in seventeen minutes! By the end of the year no less than 30,000 puzzles had been sold.

A full list of the puzzles is given in the appendix. The pictures all had some Great Western connection: about a third were of actual railway subjects, including a cut-out photograph of *King George V*, a diesel rail-car and a very interesting coloured photograph of the erecting shop at Swindon—*Locomotives in the Making*. Among the scenic views were several of Devon and Cornwall, a night scene in Piccadilly Circus, and an aerial photograph of Windsor Castle. Two puzzles had unusual features; a colour reproduction of Frith's *The Railway Station*, with a modern view of Paddington, in a twin box, issued in 1926, and a picture of Exeter cathedral by Fred Taylor, with a map of the GWR on the reverse side, dating from the same year.

The puzzles were very widely advertised in the company's books, in *Holiday Haunts* and in lists of publications, and they were frequently mentioned in the *Magazine*. The high quality combined with low price, and the appeal of the subjects—particularly those of direct railway interest—ensured great popularity for the GWR jig-saws between the issue of *Caerphilly Castle* in 1924 and the last design produced in 1937. Although the majority were bought by individuals, quantities were ordered by jig-saw clubs where the puzzles were put together in timed competitions, and they were also recommended by doctors for patients suffering from nervous disorders. Many more were passed on to hospitals and convalescent homes. They made excellent Christmas presents and sales during the Christmas period alone rose from 21,344 in 1928 to 31,404 in 1932. In December 1928 the GWR Dublin office sold no less than 554 puzzles.

Sales of individual titles were governed both by the popularity of the pictures and by the length of time particular puzzles were kept in production. 77,686 copies of the pioneer puzzle *Caerphilly Castle* were sold, and up to the end of 1933 over 35,000 each of *King George V* and *Cornish Riviera Express*, and over 30,000 of *Exeter Cathedral* had been sold. More than three-quarters of a million puzzles were sold by the company between 1924 and the end of 1935.

The production of the puzzles was mainly the responsibility of the stationery and printing department, but some of the subjects, including those adapted from Great Western posters, were suggested by the publicity department. The actual manufacture was done entirely by Chad Valley.

In addition to the forty-four jig-saw puzzles in the main series, three smaller puzzle trains for younger children were produced at the same time as a table game *Race to the Ocean Coast*, and of these smaller puzzles nearly 13,000 were sold.

Initially the puzzles were packed in cardboard boxes with lift-off lids and labels showing a reduced version of the picture as a key, and incorporating the Great Western arms, but at a later date (probably about 1934) a new book-box, designed to stand upright on a shelf, came into use. Some puzzles were issued in both types of box, and there was a larger book-box for the 500-

piece puzzles. Each box contained publicity matter about the Great Western.

Publicity for the jig-saw puzzles was reduced in the later 30s as the older titles were exhausted and fewer new ones were being produced, and they ceased to be advertised after the outbreak of the second war. The Chad Valley Company's own catalogue still listed eleven GWR puzzles in 1939, though the number of pieces had been reduced from 200 to 150, while the price remained at 2s 6d (12½p).

Sir Felix Pole stated in his memoirs that the puzzles were sold at just about cost price, so that the company was able to gain valuable publicity at little cost, while giving a great deal of amusement to countless thousands of children and adults.

COLOURED PLATES

From the earliest days of the *Great Western Railway Magazine* separate copies of the frontispiece plates were offered to readers at a nominal charge, but many of these were portraits or other subjects of interest only to the staff of the company. There is no record of the plates so issued, and it is therefore not possible to compile a complete list.

The frontispiece to the 1910 *Holiday Haunts*, depicting the 4–6–0 locomotive *King Edward* ('Star' class), was offered for sale as a 12 x 10in enlargement at 2s 6d (12½p), but this appears to be the only case in which pictures were offered for sale, although individual requests were probably met, and prints from official negatives of engines and rolling stock were supplied by the chief mechanical engineer's department at Swindon.

In later years the opportunity was taken to sell the coloured plates used for two of the jig-saw puzzles; that of *King George V* was on sale in 1928, and *The Cheltenham Flyer* was offered in 1933. Both were priced at one shilling. The former plate seems to have sold out by 1935, but the *Flyer*, which was from one of F. Moore's paintings, continued to be available until 1939.

CHILDREN'S TABLE GAME

The very successful co-operation between the Great Western

Railway and The Chad Valley Company in the production of jig-saw puzzles led to the firm manufacturing a children's game *Race to the Ocean Coast*. The game consisted of a folding board, 22 x 15in, on which was printed a picture map of the GWR system, and the players, starting from Paddington, raced to the Ocean Coast by the time-honoured process used in Snakes and Ladders. The game was packed in a colourful box bearing a picture of a 'King' at speed, and the arms of the GWR company, and it sold for half a crown.

Race to the Ocean Coast was advertised in *Holiday Haunts* for 1930, and an illustration of the box appeared in an article on the Chad Valley works in the *Magazine* for September, 1931, but it then disappears from the scene. 5,500 sets of the game were sold, which apparently did not come up to expectations, and it was discontinued.

CHILDREN'S PAINTING BOOK

The *Magazine* sometimes carried a short paragraph suggesting various Great Western publications as suitable Christmas gifts, and in December 1925 there is mention of 'a beautifully coloured painting book for children, who will love the pictures of railways . . . and will undoubtedly be glad of the opportunity of imitating them'. This was *All About Railways*, a children's painting book priced at a shilling, which had then been recently published. Like the table game, no copy is in the archives, and it is doubtful if any have survived.

PICTURE POSTCARDS
(see Appendix 4)

Although picture postcards are taken very much for granted today, they are of comparatively recent origin, and were first accepted by the Post Office as late as 1894, when the postage charged for inland transmission was a halfpenny. The cheap postage and the attraction of the cards themselves led to the very rapid rise of a new industry, and in addition to their use for ordinary messages and greetings, they also provided a new subject for collectors, and in Edwardian times picture postcard collecting became a craze.

Several railway companies issued postcards, among the first in the field being the London and North Western, who claimed to have sold over six million by 1904. The Great Western was early on the scene with its first series of twenty-five cards printed in sepia gravure and selling at a halfpenny each or a shilling (5p) the set. These, and a second series, also of twenty-five, appeared in 1904 and some of the latter were illustrated in the *Magazine* in October of that year.

The subjects in the first two series showed a wide variety, ranging from Churchward's prototype 4–6–0 engine No 98 to Eton playing fields. A third series of coloured reproductions of GWR pictorial posters was produced in 1905, and series 4, consisting mainly of views of Great Western territory, again in gravure, followed later in the year. At about the same time series 5, printed from three-colour blocks, and again depicting scenic subjects, was published at a shilling the set of twenty-five.

Two years later, in 1908, a sixth series of twelve glossy photographs of Great Western engines appeared, also at a shilling, which included the de Glehn Compound *La France* and 4002 *Evening Star*. By the end of 1909 the first four series were out of print, but in 1910 twenty-four cards (series 8) entitled *Fishguard Harbour as a Port of Call*, was issued at only sixpence (2½p) the set—another facet of the publicity campaign for the port. A number of these cards showed various views of the SS *Mauretania* at Fishguard, where she called for the first time in August 1909.

The seventh series, also issued in 1910, was advertised in *Holiday Haunts* for 1910 as 'glossy coloured reproductions from photographs of Cornish resorts'. One of these showed a view of Saltash bridge, and the whole series of twelve, which sold for sixpence the set, were very attractive and now among the scarcest of the Great Western cards.

Of four further series issued, series 9, again devoted to West Country subjects appeared about 1910, and was in the form of sepia bromide prints. After the first war series 10 and 11, both in gravure, depicted scenery and buildings in various parts of the GWR system, and the last, series 12, also in gravure, covered some of the Cathedrals in Great Western territory. The issue of these may well have coincided with the publication of the book *Cathedrals*. At a later date some were overprinted with an advertisement for the three books in that series, and supplied to booksellers, with their name and address, for use as book publicity.

The cards were on sale at principal stations and bookstalls and from the beginning were available from automatic machines at some stations. When the first series appeared early in 1904 there was such a demand that the Paddington machines had to be replenished many times in the first few days.

After 1915 no further mention was made of postcards in *Holiday Haunts*. The collecting craze was on the wane by the end of the war and only a comparatively small number of single cards appeared in post-war years. Of these, an outstanding issue was a double-size folding card in colour of *King George V*, from the same blocks as those used for the frontispiece of Chapman's *The "King" of Railway Locomotives*, published in 1928.

The Great Western hotels were provided with picture postcards; one set reproducing sketches of the Fishguard Bay, Tregenna Castle and Manor House hotels, the latter being by Charles Mayo, which were also used in advertisements for these establishments in *Holiday Haunts*. Another set, bearing the roundel monogram on the reverse, consisted of gravure cards from photographs.

The company could have exploited the possibilities of postcards to a much greater extent. In particular, more cards showing rolling stock, stations and engineering features would have been popular with the younger generation, and the quality of some series, particularly the gravure cards, was poor in comparison with those of other companies, notably the coloured issues of the pioneer LNWR.

CARRIAGE PICTURES

It may be taken as a compliment to railway publicity that there has always been a demand from a small but significant section of the public for copies of posters and other publicity matter for use as decoration or as collectors' pieces.

In 1906 a full-page announcement appeared in *Holiday Haunts* headed 'The Artistic Side of Railway Advertising—Views in

Page 144 *The changing presentation of the* GWR *Magazine:* (above left) *early large format, the cover in black on salmon-pink, 1903;* (right) *1908 cover in bright green and blue on white;* (below left) *the* Magazine *at its zenith, chocolate and cream, 1939;* (right) *Post-war austerity: the final issue for December 1947, black and white*

passenger carriages'. This went on to say that 'arrangements have been made for Fine Art Engravings to be exhibited in Great Western Railway Passenger Carriages . . .' Anticipating that some passengers would soon be writing in to Paddington with requests to buy copies, the announcement continued by offering prints, complete with sunk mount, at one shilling each.

These 'fine art engravings' were in fact gravure prints from photographs, and measured about 8 x 6in, on 16 x 12in mounts. These replaced earlier collotype and coloured views which had begun to appear in carriage compartments from the early 1880s. The gravures were first made available to the public in the early summer of 1905.

The photographs which were the constant (though not always very cheerful) companions of passengers on the Great Western almost to the last, were taken by the staff of the Photographic Section of the Engineering Department, and were used, as occasion demanded, as illustrations in the company's publications.

PICTORIAL POSTERS

Far more attractive than the dowdy sepia prints and photographs which often proved to be such dismal companions on long train journeys, were the coloured pictorial posters which the Great Western began to produce in the 1890s. In the 'General Information for Travellers' section of *Holiday Haunts* for 1910 it was stated that 'The Company's pictorial Posters have been greatly admired by the public, and in order to meet the requirements of collectors, the Company are willing to supply copies of these artistic bills at a nominal charge'.

Although the fact was seldom mentioned in the company's publicity after the first war, posters were to be purchased, when stocks were available, throughout the inter-war years. In the little *Literature of Locomotion* folders of the 1930s posters were offered at 2s 6d (12½p) for the double royal (25 x 40in) and 5s (25p) for the quad royal (50 x 40in) sizes. If more prominence had been given to the availability of the attractive posters of this period their survival in greater numbers might well have resulted.

I

Artistic Railway Advertising.

VIEWS IN GREAT WESTERN CARRIAGES.

Arrangements have been made for————

🙠 FINE ART ENGRAVINGS 🙠

to be exhibited in the GREAT WESTERN RAILWAY Passenger Carriages. The Engravings are printed on India paper, mounted on plate paper, and consist of pictures of the beautiful scenery at places served by the Great Western Line, and, for the guidance of travellers, views of the principal Hotels.

This new departure is much appreciated by lovers of fine art work, and, in order to meet public demand for these views, the Company have arranged for the sale of copies ready for framing, at the nominal charge of **1s.** each. The engraved surface is approximately eight inches by six inches, and the full size of the copies on sale, including sunk mount, is sixteen inches by twelve inches.

Illustrated Catalogue of the views is now ready, and copies can be obtained on application to the General Manager's Office, Paddington Station, London, W. Post free, 3d.————

Announcement in *Holiday Haunts*, 1907

COMPETITIONS

One of the manifestations of the new activity in the field of publicity in the years 1904-6 was an Essay Competition organised by the *Daily Mail* on behalf of the Great Western. The subject was to be a journey from Paddington to Cornwall, and a first prize of £50 was offered, with £10 and £5 for the runners-up. The winner was a Miss Moxon Browne, whose essay, 'of a very high order' was published in the newspaper on 7 November 1904. The judge was Max Pemberton, and his comments after making the journey himself, were flattering—and prophetic: '[Cornwall's] future, from the tourist's point of view, must be immense, and the Great Western Co. certainly have the finest train service in the world—and I am an old traveller'.

Far more important, however, was a competition sponsored by the *Railway Magazine* in August 1904. Under the heading 'Three Guineas for a Name for a Train', a prize of that amount was offered for the most suitable name for the new non-stop 'Limited' from Paddington to Plymouth and Penzance which commenced running on 1 July. The full-page announcement of the competition referred to the new train as 'the most important railway event of the present season', and made the point that the winner of the competition would not only get the three guineas prize, but 'his name will become known (and will be handed down to future generations of railway officers and *railwayacs*) as the originator of the title . . .'

The 1,286 entries were judged by J. C. Inglis, the general manager, and the prize was divided between Mr F. Hynam of Hampstead and Mr J. R. Shelley of Hackney, who submitted the name 'The Riviera Limited'. Presumably Inglis added 'Cornish' just to make sure that passengers for the south of France did not board the train by mistake. The title lives on after sixty-five years, but it is very doubtful if any of today's 'railwayacs' remember the two gentlemen who thought of it.

In 1905 there was another competition, this time for the best design of a monogram for the company's use, which was arranged through the art journal *The Studio*. The prize of two guineas was awarded for a design consisting of the letters GW interlaced, in a floriated style. None of the entries was particularly pleasing, at least to modern eyes, and even the winning design was only put to limited use, chiefly on auto coaches.

In 1910 the company ran its own Holiday Line Competition, in which three sets of questions were given in press advertisements, the answers to which could be found in *Holiday Haunts* or in Broadley's book *The Cornish Riviera*. There were two classes, for boys and girls up to sixteen, and for adults, and first prizes of £20 and £60 were offered in each class, with second and third cash prizes. Max Pemberton was again one of the judges, and another was Sir Arthur Quiller-Couch, the popular Cornish writer. Such was the response that one advertisement alone brought nearly 1,000 replies, and the closing day of the competition resulted in the largest post ever received at Paddington, up to that time, in response to an advertisement. The competition was praised by the *Railway Gazette* as 'one of the most notable advertising schemes ever undertaken by a railway company'.

Several competitions, mainly for the staff or their families, were conducted in the *Great Western Railway Magazine*. In 1912 there was a children's essay competition and in 1920 a prize of five guineas was offered for the best design for a poster advertising factory sites adjacent to the GWR lines. Results, apparently, were disappointing, but the prize was awarded to a member of the chief goods manager's staff.

In 1922, shortly after Felix Pole's appointment as general manager, the competition for poster designs, mentioned in Chapter 3, was held, and a year later it was the children's turn again, this time in an open competition for essays on 'What I know about railways', based on Chapman's *The 10.30 Limited*, then newly published. Again the response was large, and 25 per cent of the entries were from girls.

TEMPORARY ENQUIRY OFFICES

The Great Western Railway's local agencies and receiving offices, although to some extent involved in publicity, are outside the scope of the present book, but in the temporary enquiry offices and kiosks which the company installed at various outdoor functions up and down the country, publicity was one of the principal functions and a brief mention is therefore appropriate.

One of the earliest instances of which mention is made in the *Magazine* was in the summer of 1906 (again this significant year) when a great historical pageant was staged in the grounds of Warwick Castle, to which some 13,000 visitors travelled by GWR trains. A large tent was used, flanked by bill boards carrying time-bills, and inside a table spread with a supply of Great Western books. Pictorial posters formed a background to this modest but much appreciated display, and the company's flag flew from a mast alongside.

The Welsh National Eisteddfod held annually in various parts of the Principality, was a regular event which brought the company additional traffic. More than 60,000 people travelled by train to the 1924 event held at Pontypool, and here an octagonal wood and glass pagoda-like structure was erected.

This enterprise was not entirely confined to Great Western territory. In 1930, for instance, the company had a tent in one of the main avenues at Southport Flower Show. A more regular (and appropriate) fixture was the Bath and West Show, where in addition to having its enquiry office, the Great Western entered an exhibit in the Forestry section which won a number of medals. At the 1933 Show at Wimbledon the company displayed on a 64-foot long panel examples of equipment made from wood, and samples of English timber, totalling 128 items. These ranged from a restaurant car door, carriage roof-sticks and wheelbarrows to artificial limbs, chairs and rail keys. The exhibit that year won a first prize in its class.

Farm produce, including milk, was an important traffic on the Great Western, and for many years there were special arrangements for transporting livestock, machinery and produce to and from agricultural shows on the company's system. Special trains were run for exhibitors, and excursions for the thousands of visitors who flocked to these popular events. At all the larger shows of the present century there was an enquiry office, housed either in a tent, in the pagoda kiosk built in 1914, or in a larger wooden hut constructed for the purpose. Pictorial posters were put to good use as outside decoration, and staff from the goods department were on hand to answer farmers' enquiries. The importance of these events is shown by a photograph in the *Magazine* in 1915, where the large GWR enquiry hut at the Bath and West Show at Worcester is seen, with the company's Show staff of nineteen posed in front, some in uniform, others appropriately adorned with straw boaters.

BROADCASTING

The centenary of the company celebrated in the summer of 1935 was the occasion for a special feature programme broadcast by the BBC on the National wavelength at 8 pm on Friday 30 August, the eve of the centenary.

The programme was entitled 'The Great Western, August 1835 —August 1935. The First Hundred Years of a British Railway'. The *Radio Times* carried a two-column feature 'Outward Bound from Paddington' illustrated by four photographs, and one of Heath Robinson's cartoons from *Railway Ribaldry* was reproduced on the programme page. *The Listener*, too, gave generous coverage with a two-page article.

Like the centenary film, the programme dealt with the history of the company and the construction of the original line, but the most interesting part was undoubtedly the contributions by officials and staff from many parts of the GWR system and representing some of the diverse activities of a railway. The company's secretary, F. R. E. Davis, a signalman, footplate men, a clerk, a dining car chef—all spoke with pride and affection of the Great Western. What tales they had to tell—men like Ganger W. Hancock, who had spent the whole of his working life maintaining Box tunnel, and old Morris Froude, himself in his hundredth year, recalling 'Mr Brunel' and the Broad Gauge. His memories went back to his first job on the GWR in 1854 when, as a travelling porter, he sat in one of those 'iron coffins' on the locomotive tender. He had retired as long ago as 1898, and unfortunately died within a month of his own century in June of the following year. The critics and listeners were warm in their praise for the 'touch of genius' which gave Morris Froude the last words in the broadcast, a softly whispered 'good night'.

Homes for All

By far the greater part of Great Western publicity was aimed at the long-distance traveller, whether for business or pleasure, but one major campaign was initiated in an effort to increase suburban traffic. The company had invested a great deal of money in new lines in the first decade of the present century, including the new sections of the short route to Birmingham, and it was important that these new lines should be utilised to the highest possible degree. To this end the company began an intensive advertising campaign in 1912 to attract short-distance traffic to the main lines out of Paddington, to Reading and to High Wycombe, and to the branch lines and loops which connected them.

Unhampered by planning restrictions or green belts, London was expanding rapidly and indiscriminately into the surrounding countryside. It was therefore in the Great Western's interest to encourage businessmen to live in the outer suburbs and the towns of the Thames Valley and the Chilterns, and with this in view the first issue of a periodical was published in January 1912 with the appealing title of *Homes for All—London's Western Border-land*, in which the virtues of each district were extolled, and information given about new housing developments. Advertisements of estate agents, builders and schools were included, and, of course, full details of season ticket rates and a Business Man's Time Table for each route. This 'Residential Guide & Property Register' was in an attractive quarto format with buff-coloured covers modelled on those of *Holiday Haunts* and the Broadley books. It was very well illustrated with photographs of tree-lined avenues, riverside scenes and newly-erected houses, and there was a five-mile-to-the-inch coloured map showing GWR rail and road motor routes.

Homes for All was published quarterly, without charge. It ran to eleven issues, the last appearing in July 1914, after which publication was curtailed by the war. A similar periodical was produced for 'Birmingham's Beautiful Borderlands' from April 1913, but for this a nominal charge of a penny was made. Special emphasis was laid on the newly-opened North Warwickshire line, then mainly running through open country, which did in fact attract large-scale housing development within a very few years, and is a classic example of the direct influence of the railway upon the pattern of urban growth. The threatened closure of the line, as these words are being written, will leave large residential areas without a direct main road into Birmingham. The Birmingham *Homes for All* also ceased publication on the outbreak of the first war.

The Great Western was not alone in adopting this idea, though it was possibly the first railway to do so. At least two other companies produced similar publications, *Where to Live* was issued by the Great Northern in 1914 and *Homes in the South West Suburbs* by the LSWR in the same year.

WINDOW DISPLAYS

In London and the larger towns the facilities for advertising on hoardings and bill boards at stations were augmented by the windows of the receiving offices and agencies maintained by the Great Western. These were of particular value when they were situated in towns away from the company's own lines. Posters and maps were regularly displayed on boards in front of the premises, and in the windows. In places where the Great Western had no office of its own, agents were appointed to receive parcels for transit by GWR and these often had a bill board on which excursion and other posters were shown. Lists of these offices and agencies were given in the penny time book. Like the other railways, the GWR's posters and folders were displayed at the offices of Thomas Cook & Son and other travel agents.

The Great Western also received occasional publicity when booksellers mounted special displays of the company's publications, of which *Holiday Haunts* was often the centrepiece. The books on cathedrals, abbeys and castles were particularly suitable for sale in bookshops and some very attractive window displays were put on by the larger firms when these books were first published.

LUGGAGE LABELS AND MENU CARDS

The ordinary luggage labels, bearing the initials G.W.R. and the destination, were themselves a reminder to the passer-by of the many places served by the Great Western Railway, but there were occasions when something more attractive was required.

In 1931 a special adhesive label was issued for the Shakespeare Express (9.25 a.m. from Paddington to Stratford-upon-Avon). Printed in yellow and black, it bore a bold portrait of Shakespeare and the words SHAKESPEARE EXPRESS at the foot. The labels were affixed to all baggage in the van, and further copies were issued by ticket collectors during the journey. In 1932 passengers on *The Cheltenham Flyer* received a special four-colour label with the inscription WORLD'S FASTEST TRAIN. At the same period special labels were produced for the Cornish Riviera Express and for the company's hotels.

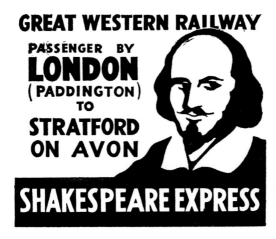

GREAT WESTERN RAILWAY

PASSENGER BY

LONDON

(PADDINGTON)

TO

STRATFORD ON AVON

SHAKESPEARE EXPRESS

Souvenir luggage label, 1931

Menu cards for use in restaurant cars and GWR hotels carried some publicity matter, either as a border or on the reverse side. The cards were printed by contract through the stationery and printing department, with a blank space for the day's bill of fare, which was inserted as required. The latter work, being required at short notice, was always done on the company's own presses at Paddington. In addition to the menu cards used by the company, in 1933 a series of thirty-eight different cards was produced carrying Holiday Season Ticket publicity, for general issue to hotels and boarding houses, and 256,000 were distributed in this way.

VISITS

Railway installations have always been popular places for visits by schoolboys and adult enthusiasts, as well as by the general public. An illustrated guide to Swindon works was published in 1929, and was also translated into French, and a revised edition, *Swindon Works and its Place in Great Western History* appeared in 1935, with a further revision in a new format in 1947. These were distributed to the many parties which toured the works on its traditional visiting day—Wednesday. For the occasional visit of our own or foreign royalty a special souvenir brochure was produced, as was the case on 28 April 1924 when King George V and Queen Mary spent over two hours at Swindon. This was the occasion when the King drove *Windsor Castle* from the works to Swindon station, with the Queen, Viscount Churchill (the chairman), Sir Felix Pole, C. B. Collett, the driver and the fireman crammed into the cab.

A handsome 16-page booklet was produced, excellently printed in sepia on cream paper, and with a cream cover bearing the arms of the GWR and of the Borough of Swindon embossed in colour. Four years later, on 21 March 1928, King Amanullah of Afghanistan and his Queen visited Swindon, and for this a similar booklet was printed, in two editions, English and Persian, with the British and Afghan flags on the covers. A menu, printed on satin, was presented to the King, and a bilingual timetable of the visit was also done.

BOOK MARKERS

A minor, but effective, advertising medium once used to a considerable extent was the printed book mark, supplied to publishers for insertion in copies of their publications. These were used in large numbers by insurance firms, and some could claim a degree of artistic merit, as for instance the series depicting the months of the year designed by Walter Crane for the Scottish Widows' Fund Life Assurance Society and issued in 1913-14.

The Great Western Railway took up the idea in the 1920s and

issued a series of 'Holiday Haunts Bookmarkers', with reproductions of sketches by Joseph Pike of Devil's Bridge, Warwick
Castle, Tintern Abbey and other landmarks on the GWR system.
They not infrequently turn up in second-hand books even today,
ready to serve their original purpose once again, though, alas, some
of the places mentioned on them can no longer be reached by train.

A book mark most often used by railway passengers—in
Bradshaw's *Guide*, sometimes carried Great Western advertisements; in the early 1920s it featured the two-hour Birmingham
expresses and the Birkenhead—Bournemouth through trains, with
the triangular 'Go Great Western' motto prominently displayed.

THE CENTRAL ENQUIRY BUREAU, PADDINGTON

The Great Western, alone among the four group companies,
included under the heading of publicity the organisation dealing
with public enquiries. A central information bureau was established at Paddington in 1928 in the office of the superintendent
of the line, and in 1932 this was reorganised and placed under
the direct control of the publicity department, and a new office
opened at No 5 Craven Street, near the station. Two years later
the bureau moved to the new building in Bishop's Bridge Road.
W. G. Chapman took charge of the bureau in 1932 and remained
until his retirement in 1940, and the work of the bureau was
described by him in two articles in the *Magazine* in October 1932
and June 1938.

The bureau handled all public enquiries previously dealt with
by various scattered departments at Paddington, including postal
and telephone enquiries, and it also despatched regular mailings
of excursion and holiday train literature amounting to about 5,000
items per month. Passenger enquiries, naturally, fluctuated according to the season, with July the busiest month. The volume of
business increased steadily from year to year. In 1932 telephone
calls were accepted for nine hours a day, weekdays only, but by
1938 the service had become available for fifteen hours, seven days
a week. In the former year 10,000 calls were received during the
four days 27-30 July, while in the week before Easter 1938 the
telephone enquiries reached 21,724, with no less than 4,932 calls

on the Thursday alone. That year brought over half a million telephone enquiries to the bureau.

Requests for information by post were an equally important part of the activities of this busy department. As many as 1,000 letters were received in a single day during busy periods, and well over 60,000 were handled in a year, of which about half required typewritten replies.

Each spring the bureau despatched some 50,000 circulars to people from whom postal enquiries had been received in the previous season, giving information on holiday travel facilities for the ensuing summer.

The second world war brought added pressure on the bureau, as it did upon other departments, and in spite of staff shortage and constant interruption by air raids, the volume of enquiries reached new high levels. In July 1944 the bureau had a record month during which 166,331 enquiries of all kinds were handled, an average of 5,365 per day, with one Friday in June bringing an all-time record of 7,402 transactions. The daily average from the outbreak of war to October 1944 was 3,600, more than double the pre-war figure.

The staff of the telephone section, from whom a very high standard of geographical and railway knowledge was expected, were specially trained for the job by means of courses lasting from three to four months, run in the bureau. In 1932 a staff of seven sufficed for telephone enquiries, but by 1938 this had doubled, with fourteen women operators, including an assistant supervisor, and a male supervisor.

Enquiries received at the bureau covered every aspect of railway passenger services, and these were by no means confined to purely Great Western lines. Many requests were received for information about trains on the other companies' lines, and on London Transport routes, and these were always answered as fully as possible. The bureau received its share of odd and amusing requests, varying from the woman whose lap-dog required a seat with its back to the engine, to the man who wished to know the number of tunnels between Paddington and Penzance.

The *Magazine* for November 1944 carried an article on the bureau and the training of its staff. The illustrations are an eloquent tribute to the way the girls maintained the service to the public during wartime air raids. A civilian-duty respirator and steel helmet hung from each girl's chair, and when the imminent danger signal was received, to quote the *Magazine*, 'each girl curls up on her little enquiry mat in the kneehole space under her desk, perches her telephone on a half pulled-out drawer, and just carries on with her service that is a blend of accurate knowledge, patience, tact, courtesy and the "smile in the voice" '.

THE STAFF'S CONTRIBUTION TO PUBLICITY

It hardly needs to be said that the front line of publicity was always the railway itself—stations, rolling stock and staff. No amount of posters and advertisements could ever be as effective as punctual, comfortable trains, clean stations and smart and courteous staff.

In the days when labour was plentiful even the smallest stations had sufficient men to keep the platforms swept clean, to polish the woodwork and the brass, and to tend the flower beds which often bordered the platforms. Many Great Western stations had bright and attractive flower beds, and some exceptionally keen staffs entered regularly for the Station Gardens Competition run by the company. These competitions originated on the Bristol & Exeter Railway as early as 1865, and the scheme was extended to the Great Western on the amalgamation in 1876.

Ingenuity was sometimes used in arranging the name of the station, or some slogan like 'Go Great Western', in flowers or stones. Not all the best displays were at country stations; a large flower bed with the words 'Travel by the G.W.R. for Business or Pleasure' in white stones, was arranged at Cradley Heath, in the heart of the Black Country, in the late 1920s, and before the 1914 war Stourbridge Town won much admiration for its fine show of over 3,500 plants incorporating the slogan 'Best Route—Engines —Scenery—G.W.R.'.

The artistic talents of the staff found a place in the publicity sphere in another direction. Every station had its blackboard for special notices, and when, as quite often happened, a porter or clerk fancied himself as an artist, the result could be publicity with a distinctly personal flavour, forming a useful link between station staff and regular passengers. Chalk posters were sufficiently numerous to prompt the GWR Social and Educational Union to run a competition in 1929, with a first prize of five pounds. The resulting designs were displayed in the general meeting room at Paddington, where they were inspected by the directors and officials and by the general public. The winner was a retired Smithfield clerk, the second prize went to a clerk from Ross, and the third to a Paddington cloak-room attendant.

The *Magazine* for September 1939 carried an article 'Posters with a Point', describing the activities of Parcels Porter S. C. Purnell at Bridport station, where he provided a regular supply of appropriate publicity for local services. His enthusiasm was perhaps not untypical of Great Western men, particularly at the smaller country stations where the staff often remained for long periods and became very much part of the local scene. Purnell had been at Bridport for ten years and was obviously something of a character—'broad and burly of stature, wears a cheery smile, and always, when flowers are to be had at all, a buttonhole', to quote the *Magazine* reporter.

When horse-drawn vehicles were in regular use they were occasionally pressed into service for yet another form of publicity in which the local station staff had an interest—as floats in the local carnival procession. This was by no means an uncommon occurrence, and occasionally the Great Western entry was awarded a prize, as at Exeter in 1932, when a float depicting a schoolroom scene with the title 'Go Great Western, a Lesson worth Learning', was judged the best tableau in the show.

MAPS OF THE GREAT WESTERN RAILWAY

The unique life-span of the Great Western Railway provides almost endless fields for study, and one of these is the evolution of railway maps from the 1830s to the 1940s. There is no shortage of accessible material from which a history of the maps could be compiled, but the subject is too large, and perhaps too specialised, to be dealt with in detail in a general survey of the company's publicity.

When the Great Western embarked on its publishing activities in 1904 various maps were used in *Holiday Haunts* and the travel books, printed by specialist map printers, notably W. & A. K. Johnston of Edinburgh, as well as by Wyman & Sons and other general printers who did work for the company. These included not only maps of the whole system, but sectional sheets covering Ireland, Brittany and areas as small as Devon or Cornwall. The penny time book in the early years of the present century contained route maps printed by Wyman not unlike the much later productions mentioned below, but these were not used in other publications.

In 1914 the eminent printer Emery Walker produced an entirely new standard map in which the land contours were printed in half-tone, in light brown, while the routes and place names were printed from a wax process which allowed the use of printing types instead of drawn lettering, making for much increased legibility and uniformity. The early Emery Walker maps, with GWR routes in rich black, were both handsome and practical.

After the grouping these maps reappeared with the routes printed in red, and soon afterwards the contour shading was dispensed with, leaving a map which continued to be produced, at first by Emery Walker and later by George Philip & Son, until 1947. The maps were regularly brought up to date by the addition of new stations and the removal of those which had closed, and a variety of large-scale insets were used as circumstances required.

The standard maps were kept in stock at the stationery and printing department and supplied to printers for insertion in publications and time books, and they were also issued to the public in a folder or envelope.

Specialised maps of many kinds were produced at various times, of which the commercial map, showing mineral deposits and coalfields, printed by W. & A. K. Johnston in 1909, was a particularly fine example. This was supplied on rollers for hanging, or folded in cloth covers. A map and index of goods stations, printed by Geographia Ltd, was issued in 1933, and the same firm produced an enlarged, quad royal, version of the standard route map, complete with roundel monogram, in the late 1930s. The standard map was also lithographed on tinplate and enclosed in a wooden frame for display on stations, and reduced (and somewhat distorted) versions were printed on card for use in passenger coaches alongside the photographic views.

Many of the booklets and pictorial folders issued between the wars contained specially prepared maps or diagrams illustrating specific holiday areas, services like country cartage and railhead distribution, and there was even a large folding map showing all the golf courses on the Great Western.

TIMETABLE AND TIME BOOKS

The preparation of timetables and time books was the responsibility of the timetable section, and as with all other printed matter, they were printed under contract through the stationery department. The publicity department was only concerned in supplying the advertisements and in distribution of time books to stations, bookstalls, hotels, ships and other outlets.

The history of railway timetables, an intricate and fascinating subject, has yet to be written, and like the evolution of maps, is outside the scope of the present survey.

Chapter 7

The *Great Western Railway Magazine*

Before discussing the development of the *Great Western Railway Magazine* which was published between 1888 and 1947, and for most of this period was the house journal of the company, there is an earlier periodical of similar name which, though not in any sense publicity, is nevertheless worthy of mention.

The magazine, or literary miscellany, was largely the creation of the nineteenth century, although a few, notably the *Gentleman's Magazine* (1731-1914) originated in the previous century. By mid-Victorian times the number of these publications had grown considerably and from the 1850s a flood of new titles appeared, including *Household Words*, conducted by Charles Dickens, and *Cornhill Magazine*, edited by W. M. Thackeray.

The vogue for these periodicals, and the initial success many of them enjoyed, encouraged the publication of minor imitations of local or sectional interest, many of them produced by amateurs, and all of them short-lived. Among these were at least two which originated in railway circles, possibly the first being the *Great Northern Journal* which appeared about 1860. In July 1862 the first number of *The Great Western Magazine* was published, with the sub-title 'A Miscellany of Fact and Fiction'. This was in the same octavo format as most of its contemporaries of which the *Cornhill*, started in 1860, was then enjoying great popularity.

The *Magazine* was 'printed and published for the Proprietors' by George Burns & Co, Steam Printers, 94 Grand Junction Terrace, Edgware Road—a singularly appropriate title and address for the printer of a railway periodical. The first issue contained thirty-two pages of text, with additional pages of advertisements, and light brown paper covers of which all but the front also carried advertisements. The price was fourpence a copy, and it seems that advertisements were forthcoming in sufficient numbers to allow the magazine to pay its way. In October it had grown to forty pages as a result of 'the very great amount of support'. Two thousand copies of the August issue were sold, and in January 1863 the secretary was appealing for the return of copies of the first issue to satisfy demands for back numbers.

The contributors were all anonymous, and even the editor failed to divulge his identity. The *Magazine* was conducted by a committee of five GWR officials of whom one, and possibly the leading light, was Ammon Beasley, who, thirty years later became general manager of the Taff Vale Railway. The committee contributed some of the articles, but others were accepted from writers not in the Great Western service. The editorial of the first issue expressed the hope that the *Magazine* would become 'in time, the recognised organ of all the Great Western servants', and although this goal was never reached, the paper was not entirely devoid of railway matters. From the first issue it contained an article headed 'The Month on the Rail' in which the affairs of the GWR and other companies were discussed. The first of these mentioned that 'the Metropolitan is making rapid strides towards completion . . .' and in December 1862 comment on the Midland company's plans to build a line from Mangotsfield to Bath left the reader in no doubt as to the editorial policy: 'The Midland Company, who have hitherto prided themselves on their keeping-within-bounds policy—than which a wiser could not be conceived—are contemplating a raid into the territory of their neighbours . . .' Railway politics were well aired in the columns of the *Railway Times* and other journals of the day, but it is a pity that this Great Western venture was so short-lived, for the opinions of its contributors over a longer period would have been a valuable addition to the recorded history of the company.

But even in its short life this early magazine did achieve one notable success, or so it was later claimed by one of its 'conductors'—probably Ammon Beasley. It was in the pages of this journal that the suggestion was first made of Staff Superannuation and Guarantee Funds, both of which later came to fruition.

The early success, as so often happened with this kind of periodical, was not maintained, and after the issue for June 1864 it ceased publication. Whether this was due to dwindling support from subscribers and advertisers, or whether the proprietors wearied of their task, is not clear, but the latter may well have been the case, for one of them, writing many years later, said of the journal's demise that 'we felt it a relief to lay down our pens'.

Twenty-four years were to elapse before the appearance of another literary enterprise connected with the Great Western, and this, again, was not sponsored by the company itself. In 1888 some of the leading members of the GWR Temperance Union, with the support of one of the directors, Lord Lyttelton, launched a new journal with the dual purpose of furthering the aims of the Temperance Union and acting as a link between the railway's 40,000-odd employees scattered throughout the system.

Lord Lyttelton, in his address to the readers in the first issue of November 1888, said that there was to be no meddling with politics, but nothing was to be excluded which would 'inform their [the staff's] minds, quicken their sympathies, and elevate and purify their lives'. High aims indeed, though quite characteristic of the times.

It is all too easy to deride the temperance movement which was so strong at that time. Drunkenness had been a terrible scourge in the early nineteenth century, particularly in London and the big towns, and the dire consequences which could result from railwaymen being intoxicated while on duty were an added spur to the supporters of temperance among railwaymen.

The first issue of the *Great Western Magazine, and Temperance Union Record* was published in November 1888, and it consisted of twelve pages, 11 x 8½in, enclosed in salmon-pink wrappers carrying advertisements. The principal contents were an article on the electric telegraph by C. E. Spagnoletti, a short biography of Lord Lyttelton (of whom a portrait was included), a page devoted to the finances and traffic receipts of the Great Western, staff changes and 'Railway Scraps', and a page headed 'Etc.' which consisted mainly of *bons mots* from other journals. The remaining pages carried news of the Temperance Union, Widows' and Orphans' Fund and the New Swindon Mechanics' Institution.

The *Magazine* can claim to be the first publication of its kind. Although the *South Western Gazette* antedates it by eight years, this latter was in newspaper form and was mainly concerned with the South Western Orphanage. It was reconstituted in magazine style as the *South Western Magazine* in 1915. Among other early railway staff journals were the *Great Central Journal* (1905), the *North Eastern Railway Magazine, Great Eastern Railway Magazine* and LNWR *Gazette*, all of which first appeared in 1911.

In succeeding years the contents of the *Great Western Railway Magazine* remained much the same, its principal purpose being to report the affairs of the increasing number of welfare organisations on the GWR, and such activities as ambulance classes, sports and staff dinners. Staff changes, retirements and obituaries were well to the fore, and there were regular contributions on aspects of railway work, including a series by C. E. Richardson on the Severn Tunnel.

The first editor was J. K. Skellern, of the Paddington goods staff, who did the work in his spare time and was unpaid. The paper was printed at the Carlton Press, Westbourne Park, where the editorial office was situated. Distribution was arranged through agents appointed at various stations on the Great Western. The *Magazine* did not get off to a very promising start, and sales of the first number were little more than 2,000, which represented the total membership of the Temperance Union, but by the end of 1888 they had risen to 7,000 copies.

The size of the *Magazine* remained much the same for many years. The price from the outset was one penny per issue, one shilling per annum, to the staff, or two shillings by post to outside subscribers. The illustrations were wood engravings taken from photographs, and lithographed plates. Separate copies of the lithographs, mainly portraits and views, were available at fourpence each, reduced to threepence in July 1889. At the end of the first volume subscribers were advised that they could have their copies 'neatly bound in cloth' for two shillings (10p).

After just a year the *Magazine* had the sad task of recording the death of Sir Daniel Gooch, which it did in a long article extending to three black-bordered pages. It could be said that the obituaries, both in these early years and later, form one of its most valuable features, giving as they do much information about the careers of railwaymen of all grades, some of whom, like Gooch, started work on the Great Western in its very early years.

The sub-title *Temperance Union Record* was dropped after two years, but the Union and other staff matters continued to predominate and only very gradually was the scope of the paper broadened to include a larger proportion of articles of general railway interest. The end of the broad gauge was fully covered in 1892 and three years later an article on early GWR locomotives sparked off a series of letters from some very familiar writers—'G. A. Sekon', Henry Greenly and Clement Stretton. The illustrations improved after 1892 when wood engravings began to give way to half-tone reproductions, and some good plates of engines were included in the 90s. But the *Magazine* still remained very much a vehicle for staff news, with little to attract the outside reader, and at the turn of the century sales had dropped to a very low level, falling to only 2,500 copies early in 1903.

At this time the Temperance Union's affairs were themselves at a low ebb and the paper's future was in the balance. The story of the transfer of the *Magazine* from the Union to the company is told in some detail by Sir Felix Pole in his autobiography. The Temperance Union, having taken over two of the GWR Coffee Tavern Company's branches which had been losing money, soon found themselves in debt, and the president, who was also deputy chairman of the Great Western company, was served with a writ. The situation called for drastic measures, and the company lent the Union £750 to clear its debt. At the same time the future of the *Magazine* was being reviewed and the company decided to cancel the Union's debt and take over the paper, a bargain of which the Union certainly had the better half. Pole, then a young junior in the chief engineer's office, saw in the post of editor a chance to make a name for himself, and after considerable lobbying among influential friends, he was offered the job as the first paid editor at an annual salary of £50, at the same time being transferred to the general manager's office.

Just as he had envisaged, Pole found in the *Magazine* an ideal means of demonstrating to his superiors the talents which he undoubtedly possessed. He took over the editorship in August 1903, and in the very next issue he introduced changes, including a new opening page of 'Railway Notes', and in February 1904 he endeared himself to the railway enthusiasts of the day by publishing the first of a series of lists of locomotive names and numbers. At the same time the distribution of the *Magazine*, which remained priced at a penny, was overhauled, new agents at stations being appointed to boost sales.

The results must have exceeded even Felix Pole's wildest hopes. When he took over the reins the circulation had fallen to 2,000 copies per month; by January 1904 sales had risen to 7,000, and by May they totalled 11,000 copies. By 1906 the popularity of the paper had already justified the faith which the company had placed in its young and ambitious editor, for in that year no less than 20,000 copies were being sold each month.

The page size was reduced in January 1905 to the more manageable format which it retained to the end, and in the same year an art edition printed on art paper was made available at twopence. By that time the *Magazine* had assumed the style which it retained, with minor alterations, throughout the remaining forty-two years.

The complete series of *Great Western Railway Magazines* form a fascinating and quite unique storehouse of facts, figures and anecdotes covering every conceivable aspect of GWR affairs. Few developments of any importance escaped notice in its pages, and the information relating to the movement, promotion and work of the staff, which always remained an important part of the paper's contents, form a valuable source of biographical material. It would be futile to attempt even the broadest summary of the contents of the 709 issues, and it therefore only remains to mention briefly some of the principal landmarks in the editorship and general progress of the paper.

Felix Pole remained in the editor's chair for nearly fifteen years, but this time was not spent solely on *Magazine* work, which was still very much a part-time job. Such had been his progress in the general manager's office that by 1919, when C. E. Aldington was appointed general manager, Pole was given the post of assistant at the early age of 42, and his place as editor was taken by Edward S. Hadley, a name later to become almost synonymous with that of the *Magazine* which he served with such distinction for eighteen years. Hadley had had twenty years service in the traffic department, latterly as chief clerk to the assistant divisional superintendent at Newport, where he introduced a new system of freight train control later adopted throughout the system. He was contributing articles to the *Magazine* as early as 1904, and in 1912 he was transferred to the general manager's office and attached to the *Magazine* staff. It was in the following year that Hadley embarked on a campaign to reduce accidents among the staff, and it is perhaps as the inventor of the 'Is it Safe?' slogan, and of the pocket tokens which were an important part of the campaign which he commenced in 1913, that he is best remembered. Not only was the safety movement responsible for saving many lives, and for a reduction of injuries, on the Great Western, but the idea soon spread to other main-line railways.

Hadley wrote a number of manuals for staff use, and was instrumental in the creation of the Social and Educational Union and the Helping Hand Fund. One of his many ideas had a direct bearing on Great Western train running. This was the All Line Goods Train Competition, introduced in 1927, and a similar scheme for passenger trains which followed two years later. The aim was to improve efficiency in loading, shunting and running by awarding points to each division based on a month's statistics, the divisions competing for a shield awarded by the *Magazine*.

Edward Hadley's term as editor spanned the inter-war years which saw some of the Great Western's finest achievements, and their coverage in the company's house journal (which by then it had become) owed much to his enthusiasm and energy. Much of his own writing was based on personal experience, and before writing on an unfamiliar topic he would spend a week or so working with a permanent way gang or other group to 'find out for himself'—a practice viewed with some suspicion by the men concerned.

Under Pole and Hadley the *Magazine*'s circulation rose steadily, subscribers coming from among people outside the railway service as well as from the company's employees, and copies found their way to many parts of the world where it was read by former Great Western men serving with foreign and colonial railways. By 1909 the circulation had reached 25,000 copies each month.

The price of the ordinary edition remained at a penny until wartime conditions necessitated a rise to twopence, and to three-pence for the art edition, in June 1918, but these increases were short-lived, lasting only until the end of 1921, and the price was never again raised. While the modest price remained constant, readers were getting more and more for their money, almost every successive year showing an increase in the number of pages and a larger proportion of illustrations. In 1905 the year's issues totalled 226 pages. This had grown to 360 in 1912 and jumped to 404 in 1913. The war necessitated a considerable reduction in the size of the *Magazine*, but by 1922 the upward trend was resumed with an annual total of 570 pages. In post-war years the size fluctuated considerably, but readers were always sure of between 450 and 550 pages per year, and when more prosperous times returned the annual volumes were in the region of 600 pages. The centenary issue, for September 1935, with 103 pages, was the largest single issue ever published, and that year totalled 682 pages. It is a gross understatement to say that the *Magazine* was a very good penny-worth indeed. Little wonder that the circulation had reached 44,000 copies by the end of 1937.

In addition to the ordinary and art editions, a scheme was intro-duced in 1912 by which the staff could pay an extra penny per issue for the Insurance Edition, and by so doing become eligible for cash payments in the event of injury or death. The scheme was only applicable to regular subscribers, and the only dis-tinguishing feature of this edition was the words Insurance Edition printed on the cover.

In 1937, after seeing the April issue through the press, Edward Hadley retired, having served the Great Western for forty-seven years, and the *Magazine* as contributor and editor for thirty-three years. His successor as editor was R. F. Thurtle, who had been on the editorial staff since 1927. His association with the *Magazine* had begun while he was station master at Pontrilas, when he con-tributed articles which came to the notice of the general manager, Sir Felix Pole, who had him transferred to Paddington to assist Hadley. One of his first acts as editor was to abandon the long-standing practice of having advertisements on the front cover. From January 1938 an attractive pictorial cover was introduced, printed on cream-tinted paper, which greatly improved the appearance of the paper. Unfortunately a reduction in the number of pages was found necessary at this time, and this trend was greatly accelerated when war came again and paper was rationed. The lowest ebb was reached in 1943 when the year's issues contained only 192 pages. During the second war the *Magazine* played a valuable part in maintaining morale among the staff and in creating a link with the many GWR men serving in the armed forces.

On 2 June 1942 the editor collapsed in the office and died shortly afterwards. R. F. Thurtle was a gifted writer and his ambitious plans for the *Magazine* had to be severely curtailed through the difficulties of wartime. The new editor, Charles Beaumont, came from the publicity department, where he was in charge of the production of *Holiday Haunts* and pictorial posters. His appointment as editor was made in February 1943, and his tenure of office proved tragically short, for he was injured during an air raid while on civil defence duties, and died on 31 March 1944.

The publicity department again provided a successor in W. H. M. Woodley, who went to Paddington from the West Country in 1941 to join the press bureau. The last three volumes appeared under his editorship and he continued as editor of the *Western Region Magazine* until his retirement in 1958.

Although the war was over, paper shortage restricted the size of the *Magazine* in 1946-7 and the fuel crisis resulted in the first and only break in continuity, with only eleven issues appearing in the latter year. With the impending nationalisation it was hardly to be expected that there would be any major developments in the form or contents of the paper in these last years.

The cover of the January 1947 issue reproduced the cartoon which appeared in the *South Wales News* in November 1922, just before the Railways Act of 1921 came into force, with the caption 'The Great Western: "Hooray, Never even blew me cap off!" ', and the editorial comment voiced the anxiety over the company's future which was felt at that time: 'Many members of the company's staff will be asking themselves how its prestige and its old familiar title will be affected by the events of 1947'.

From February the covers carried a series of photographs of

Great Western men at work, under the title 'Pride in the Job', but in them was more than a hint of sadness and uncertainty as to the future of 'the old company'. On the cover of the last issue, for December 1947, was a photograph in this series of the general manager, Sir James Milne, and a melancholy list of retirements filled the inside pages. As if to symbolise the end of an era, the last page contained an offer of back numbers dating right back to 1888, and a note that 'we hope to publish monthly as hitherto' in 1948. The mood of the *Magazine* was summed up in a poem by N. Ross Murray, with the title 'Goodbye, Great Western', the last stanza of which makes a fitting epilogue to this account of one small part of the company's activities during its one hundred and twelve years:

> Alas! the curtain falls, the lights are low:
> Pride of Brunel, now it is time to go;
> But when old days are dim, when we have gone,
> May all thy grand traditions still live on.

So be it.

1911 advertisement for **The Great Western Magazine**

Check List of Sale Publications

The Great Western was none too careful in the bibliographical details printed on the title-pages of its publications, and information from advertisements and notices in the *Magazine* are similarly unreliable. In the following check list, where the month and year of publication are shown on the recto or verso of the title-page these are printed thus : 6/1905. Where the year only is printed, but the month has been established from other sources (often from subsequent editions) the month appears in square brackets thus : [6/]1905. Where the book is undated, but the year of publication is known, this appears in square brackets.

All prices are for the paper-bound edition in which almost all GWR books were published. Prices in parentheses, eg (2s 6d), are for cloth-bound editions. It has not been possible to ascertain whether or not certain editions of some books were issued in cloth bindings, and it is quite possible that some were not, as the cheaper version may well have sold out, necessitating a reprint or new edition, while stocks remained of the bound version.

It is important that a clear distinction be made between the bound editions listed here and the books and booklets provided with cloth or leather binding cases for use in hotels, ships and clubs, and for presentation. These latter may be distinguished by the fact that in most cases the original paper or card cover is retained and the case merely glued on, and by the style of binding, which was in a dark red, rough-grained cloth or dark red roan (cheap leather). The gilt was often of poor quality and would now be tarnished.

In a very few cases no date or price is shown in this list as no copy of, or reference to, the particular edition has been traced.

No	Title	Author	Editions	Date	Price
1	The Cornish Riviera	[A. M. Broadley]	1	1904	3d
2			2	1905	3d (2s 6d)
3			3	1908	3d
4			4	6/1914	3d (2s 6d)
5			5	1924	6d
6			2nd issue[1]	1926	6d
7	Historic Sites and Scenes of England	[A. M. Broadley]	1	7/1904	3d
8			2[2]	3/1905	1s (leather 2s 6d)
9			3	8/1910	3d (2s 6d)
10			4	6/1924	6d
11	Southern Ireland. Its Lakes and Landscapes	[A. M. Broadley]	1	1904	3d
12			2	1906	3d (2s 6d)
13	South Wales. The Country of Castles	[A. M. Broadley]	1	6/1905	3d (2s 6d)
14			2	12/1907	3d (2s 6d)
15			3	1914	3d (2s 6d)
16			4	8/1924	6d
17	North Wales. The British Tyrol	[A. M. Broadley]	1	8/1906	3d (2s 6d)
18			2	7/1911	3d (2s 6d)
19			3	6/1924	6d
20	Devon. The Shire of the Sea Kings	[A. M. Broadley]	1	11/1906	3d (2s 6d)
21			2	3/1908	3d
22			3	5/1912	3d (2s 6d)
23			4	3/1916	3d

No	Title	Author	Editions	Date	Price
24			5	3/1926	6d
25			5 2nd imp	5/1908	6d
26	The Cathedral Line of England, Its Sacred Sites and Shrines	[A. M. Broadley]	1		3d
27	Wilts, Somerset and Dorset. Wonderful Wessex	[A. M. Broadley]	1	6/1908[3]	6d
28	Rural London. The Chalfont Country and the Thames Valley	[A. M. Broadley]	1	5/1909	3d
29			2	4/1924	6d
30	Beautiful Brittany	[A. M. Broadley]	1	1909[4]	
31			2	8/1910	6d
32	Cornwall and its Wild Life		1		
33			2	7/1911	1d
34	Great Western Railway. Names of Engines		1	1911[5]	6d
35	Great Western Railway Engines	A. J. L. W[hite]	2	1914	6d
36	Great Western Railway Engines	A. J. L. W[hite]	3	1917	1s
37	Names, Numbers, Types and Classes	,,	4	1919	1s
38		,,	5	1922	1s
39		,,	6	1923	1s
40		,,	7	1925	1s
41		,,	8	1926	1s

No	Title	Author	Editions	Date	Price
42		A. J. L. W[hite]	9	1928	1s
43		"	10	1929	1s
44	The G.W.R. Engine Book		1	1932[6]	1s
45			2	1932	1s
46	The Engine Book		1	1935	1s
47	GWR Engines. Names, Numbers, Types & Classes	W. G. C[hapman]	1	1938	1s
48			2	1938	1s
49			3	1939	1s
50			4	1946	1s
51	Haunts and Hints for Anglers		1	1914	6d
52	Haunts and Hints for Anglers Sea Angling		1	1925	1s
53	Haunts and Hints for Anglers Fresh Water Angling		1	1925	1s
54	War Record of the Great Western Railway	Edwin A. Pratt	1	1922[7]	1s
55	The Cambrian Coast	'Lyonesse' [G. B. Barham]	1	1922	6d
56	Legend Land. Volume I		1	1922	6d
57	Legend Land. Volume II		1	1922	6d
58	The 10.30 Limited	W. G. Chapman	1	[8/]1923	1s
59		"	2	9/1923	1s
60			3	11/1923	1s

No	Title	Author	Editions	Date	Price
61	Legend Land. Volume III	'Lyonesse' [G. B. Barham]	4	2/1924[8]	1s
62	Legend Land. Volume IV	"	1	1923	6d
63	Cathedrals	[G. E. Beer]	1	1923	6d
64			1	[3/1924][9]	2s 6d
65			2	7/1925	2s 6d (5s)
66			2 2nd imp	2/1926	(5s)
67	"Caerphilly Castle"	W. G. Chapman	1	[8/]1924	1s
68			2nd imp	9/1924	1s
69			3rd imp	9/1924	1s
70			4th imp	9/1924	1s
71	Cotswold Ways	F.V.M.	1	[6/1924][10]	6d
72	Through the Window. I Paddington to Penzance		1	1924[11]	1s
73	Abbeys	M. R. James	2nd imp	1927[12]	1s
74			2	1939[13]	6d
75			1	[8/]1925	(5s)
76			2nd imp	2/1926	(5s)
77	Brunel and After	Archibald Williams	1	1925	1s
78	"Somerset Ways"		1	[c 1924-6][10]	6d
79			2	5/1928[14]	6d
80	Through the Window. II Paddington to Birkenhead		1	1925[15]	1s
81	Through the Window. III Paddington to Killarney		1	1926[15]	1s

No	Title	Author	Editions	Date	Price
82	Castles	Charles Oman	1	1926	(5s)
83	The Channel Islands		1	1927[16]	6d
84	Twixt Rail and Sea	W. G. Chapman	1	1927[17]	1s
85	History of the Great Western Railway. Vol I Part 1, Part 2	E. T. MacDermot	1	1927	(21s 2 parts)
86	The Cornish Riviera	S. P. B. Mais	1	[8/]1928	1s (2s 6d)
87			2	[4/]1929	1s (2s 6d)
88			2 2nd imp	[6/]1932[18]	1s (2s 6d)
89			3	2/1934	1s (2s 6d)
90	Glorious Devon	S. P. B. Mais	1	[8/]1928	1s (2s 6d)
91			2	[4/]1929	1s (2s 6d)
92			2 2nd imp	[6/]1932[18]	1s (2s 6d)
93			3	2/1934	1s (2s 6d)
94	The "King" of Railway Locomotives	W. G. Chapman	1	9/1928	1s
95			2nd imp	9/1928	1s
96	Locomotives of the Great Western Railway		1	[1929][19]	1s
97	Pembrokeshire and South West Wales	A. G. Bradley	1	1930	6d
98	History of the Great Western Railway. Volume II	E. T. MacDermot	1	1931	(10s 6d)
99	Rambles in the Chiltern Country	Hugh E. Page	1	1931	6d
100			2		6d
101			3	1931	6d

No	Title	Author	Editions	Date	Price
102	Southern Ireland	Maxwell Fraser	4	1937	6d
103	Rambles in Shakespeare Land and the Cotswolds	Hugh E. Page	1	1932	6d
104			1	1933	6d
105	Rambles in South Devon	Hugh E. Page	2	1938[20]	6d
106			1		
107			2	1933	6d
108	Cheltenham Flyer	W. G. Chapman	1	[8/]1934	1s
109			2nd imp	[10/]1934	1s
110			3rd imp	2/1935	1s
111	Cornwall at Work	Ashley Brown	1	1934	1s
112	Somerset	Maxwell Fraser	1	1934	1s (2s 6d)
113			2	1934[21]	1s (2s 6d)
114	Railway Ribaldry	W. Heath Robinson	1	[5/]1935[22]	1s
115	Track Topics	W. G. Chapman	1	[7/]1935	1s
116			2	[12/]1935	1s
117			3	5/1939	1s
118	Rambles and Walking Tours in Somerset	Hugh E. Page	1	1935	6d
119			2	1938[20]	6d
120	Loco's of "The Royal Road"	W. G. Chapman	1	1936	1s
121	North Pembrokeshire. A Book for Hikers	E. Roland Williams	1	1936	6d
122	Rambles Around the Cambrian Coast	Hugh E. Page	1	1936[20]	6d

No	Title	Author	Editions	Date	Price
123	Rambles and Walking Tours in The Wye Valley	Hugh E. Page	1	1938[20]	6d
124	Rambles and Walking Tours in South Devon	Hugh E. Page	1	1939	6d
125	Dunkirk and the Great Western	Ashley Brown	1	[1945]	1s
126	Walks Around St Ives, Cornwall	Hugh E. Page	1	1946	6d
127	Next Station	Christian Barman	1	1947[23]	5s
128	Swindon Works and its Place in Great Western History		see note 24	1947	2s 6d
129	Walks Around Manor House Hotel, Near Moretonhampstead, Devon	Hugh E. Page	1	1947	6d
130	Motoring from Manor House Hotel	Kent Karslake	1	1947	6d
131	From Cave Man to Roman in Britain	Edward J. Burrow	1	n.d.	6d
132	Extracts from the Diary of Mr George Henry Gibbs	Introd by Lord Aldenham	1	n.d.[25]	6d

Notes

1   1926 issue was reset in larger type.
2   The early history of this title is confused, but the second edition was probably a special one for America and may have run concurrently with the smaller first edition.
3   There is mention of a second edition being prepared in 1916, but no copy has been traced and publication may have been abandoned owing to the war.
4   This edition had text in French and English.
5   Editions from 1911 to 1929 were published by the *Great Western Railway Magazine*, the remainder by the company.
6   The first edition with pictorial cover. No 45 had a circular cut-out cover, and an erratum slip on page 32. No 46 had a normal cover and the error corrected.
7   Published by Selwyn & Blount Ltd, but distributed by the *Magazine*.
8   Title-page reads 'published 1923'.
9   The first edition had no folding map at the end which was included in later editions. The second edition of the paper-covered version had a blue and yellow cover, possibly because the cream cover of the first edition was too easily soiled. The architectural section was by Martin S. Briggs.
10   Published by Simpkin, Marshall Ltd in conjunction with the GWR.
11   Compiled and produced by Edward J. Burrow Ltd, Cheltenham, for the company. Plain cover.
12   As last item, but coloured pictorial cover.
13   Published by the company, in a new format.
14   Larger format, published by the company.
15   Compiled and produced by Edward J. Burrow Ltd, Cheltenham, for the company.
16   Published jointly by GWR and Southern Railway.
17   Published by H. N. Appleby Ltd, London and Cardiff, in conjunction with the GWR.
18   No copy identified. Second impression probably not stated on the verso of title-page.
19   Oblong format. Twelve gravure plates and printed tissues. Reissued in 1932 at sixpence with 'Price 6d' either rubber-stamped or printed on cover.
20   Copies sold during the second war had a red-printed slip concerning wartime conditions on half-title.
21   Second edition is only identifiable by the bibliography added at the end of the book.

22 A small number was issued in decorated cloth boards for presentation only.

23 Published by Allen & Unwin Ltd for the GWR.

24 The previous edition of 1935 bore no price and was not advertised for sale.

25 Published serially in the *Magazine*, 1909-10, and subsequently published in booklet form by the *Magazine*.

The booklets in this series were more akin to the sale publications than to the great mass of other free literature. They appeared at about the period of the first war, but the dates of the first editions have not been ascertained with the exception of *Places of Pilgrimage* which appeared in the series in 1915, although it had previously been published in 1913. The majority of surviving copies seen are dated in the period 1923-7. They are often found in the red cloth or leather bindings in which they were supplied for use in ships, clubs etc.

Each book has a series number on the title-page.

1   The Cornish Riviera. Its Scenery, Attractions and Historical Associations.
2   Devon. The Lovely Land of the 'Mayflower'.
3   Shakespeare-Land. The World's Great Travel Shrine.
4   Wonderful Wessex. The Homeland of Thomas Hardy, William Barnes, and John Lothrop Motley.
5   Places of Pilgrimage for American Travellers. The Travel Shrines of the West and how best to visit them.
6   The Wye Valley II. From Hereford to Chepstow.
7   The Severn Valley. Through the Land of the Lord Marchers from Shrewsbury to Worcester.
8   Cornwall and its Wild Life.
9   The Wye Valley I. Its Stately Castles, Matchless Ruins [etc] from Plynlimon to Hereford.
10   Southern Ireland, its Lakes and Landscapes.*
11   The Cader Country : How to Explore it.

*Booklet No. 10 in an official GWR Magazine advertisement states the title as Welsh Mountain Railway, which was published, so the list in fact made 12 titles in total.

FREE BOOKLETS

In addition to the 'Handy Aids' series, these booklets were advertised with the sale publications in the 1920s. Some titles are also found in the red cloth or leather bindings. The booklets are not uniform in size.

Winter Resorts on the G.W.R.
Camping Holidays on the G.W.R.
Cardigan Bay Resorts
The Ocean Coast
Inland and Marine Spas
Wessex White Horses
Golf Courses served by the G.W.R.
The Glories of the Thames
Sunny Cornwall

CATHEDRAL GUIDE SERIES

This series of guide books to cathedrals, in foolscap octavo format, were originally published by J. M. Dent & Sons Ltd. Some or all of the stock was taken over by the GWR about 1931. They were advertised in *Holiday Haunts* for that year, and elsewhere for a short time, after which they disappear from the company's list. These little books each contained about 200 pages of letterpress, had a photogravure frontispiece and many illustrations in half-tone and line. They were all priced at 2/6d for the cloth boards and in paper covers at 1/- (except The Westminster Abbey publication).

1   St. Pauls and Southwark *by E. Beresford, H. E. Powell Jones and Edward Foord*
2   Westminster Abbey *by Beatrice Home*
3   Bristol, Bath and Malmesbury *by Gordon Home and Edward Foord*
4   Winchester and Salisbury *by Edward Foord*
5   Wells, Glastonbury and Cleeve *by Edward Foord*
6   Exeter, Truro and The West *by Edward Foord*
7   Gloucester, Tewkesbury and District *by Edward Foord*
8   Hereford and Tintern *by Edward Foord*
9   Worcester, Malvern and Birmingham *by J. Penderel-Brodhurst*
10 Oxford and Neighbourhood *by Cecil Headlam*
11 Chester, Manchester and Liverpool *by Beatrice Home*
12 St. David's, Llandaff and Brecon *by Edward Foord*

Check List of Jig-saw Puzzles

The jig-saw puzzles were manufactured by The Chad Valley Co Ltd, of Harborne, Birmingham. The subjects were chosen by the Stationery & Printing or Publicity Departments of the GWR, and some were adapted from pictorial posters.

It has not been possible to trace specimens of all the puzzles, and as only the titles were usually given in advertisements the names of the artists and the dimensions of the puzzles have had to be omitted from this list. The dates of issue shown here (with the exception of *Caerphilly Castle*) are the earliest dates on which individual puzzles have been found in the company's advertisements or in surviving Chad Valley catalogues.

Also advertised in the 1927 GWR Magazine were three small puzzles for the younger children. They were:-

No	Title	Price	Date
1	King George V (Engine)	2s 6d	1927
2	GWR Passenger Coach	2s 6d	1927
3	Combined Engine and Coach	2s 6d	1927

The advertisement read 'The Great Western Railway have produced a most attractive novelty in the form of model "puzzle trains". These, while retaining the main features of the jig-saw series, are not difficult to erect, and have the additional attraction for children of possessing real runners and therefore being mobile when complete. Each puzzle is complete in itself, and represents a handsome and lasting toy'.

No	Title	Approx. No. of Pieces	Price	Date
1	Caerphilly Castle	150[1]	2s 6d[2]	1924
2	Exeter Cathedral	250	2s 6d	1926
	Map of GWR on reverse side			
3	St Julien (three-quarter view)	150	2s 6d	1926
4	St Julien (side view)	250	2s 6d	
5	Windsor Castle	150	2s 6d	1926
6	The Railway Station (Frith)	see		
	View of Paddington Station	note[3]	2s 6d	1926
7	King George V	250	2s 6d	1928
		300	3s 6d	1928
8	Britain's Mightiest	250	2s 6d	1928
9	Swansea Docks	250	2s 6d	1928
10	Oxford	250	2s 6d	1928
11	Speed	150	2s 6d	1928
12	Cornish Riviera Express	250	2s 6d	1929[4]

No	Title	No. of Pieces	Price	Date
13	The Freight Train	150	2s 6d	1928
14	Ann Hathaway's Cottage	250	2s 6d	1930
15	A Cornish Fishing Village	250	2s 6d	1930
16	Glorious Devon	250	2s 6d	1930
17	Springtime in Devon—Fingle Bridge	250	2s 6d	1930
18	The Vikings landing at St Ives	375	5s	1930
19	St David's Cathedral	250	2s 6d	1930
20	Warwick Castle	250	2s 6d	1930
21	Torbay Express	375	5s	1930
22	Mountains of Killarney	150	2s 6d	1932
23	Windsor Castle	150	2s 6d	1932
24	King Arthur on Dartmoor	375	5s	1933
25	Stratford-upon-Avon—Harvard House	375	5s	1933
26	Beau Nash's Bath	150	2s 6d	1933
27	Henley Bridge	200	2s 6d	1933
28	Historic Totnes	200	2s 6d	1933
29	Piccadilly Circus	200	2s 6d	1933
30	The Romans at Caerleon	200	2s 6d	1933
31	The Royal Route to the West	200	2s 6d	1933
32	Oxford—Brasenose College	400	5s	1933
33	The Cheltenham Flyer	150	2s 6d	1933
34	Locomotives Old and New	200	2s 6d	1934
35	Stratford-upon-Avon	400	5s	1934
36	Sir Francis Drake at Plymouth[5]	400	5s	1934
37	The Model Railway	200	2s 6d	1935
38	The Night Mail	200	2s 6d	1935
39	London Highways	200	2s 6d	1935
40	Fishguard Army, 1797	200	2s 6d	1935
41	Streamline Way	200	2s 6d	1935
42	Windsor Castle from the Air	200	2s 6d	1937
43	Great Western Locomotives in the Making	200	2s 6d	1937
44	Cornwall—Preparing for a Catch	200	2s 6d	1937

Notes

1 Later increased to 200 pieces
2 5s for approximately one month, then reduced to 2s 6d
3 Twin puzzles in special box (250 pieces)
4 The painting used for this puzzle is dated 1929, but the title appears in advertisements during the previous year. A possible explanation is that there were two puzzles of this title, but no evidence has been found of this
5 Title changed to *Drake Goes West* in 1935
   Nos 27, 28, 30, 31, 34, 37, 40, 42, 43 and 44 were reduced to 150 pieces in 1939

APPENDIX 3

Check List of Lantern Slide Lectures

GREAT WESTERN RAILWAY
LANTERN LECTURES

THE GREAT WESTERN RAILWAY (Publicity Department) have numerous sets of Lantern Lectures covering the territory served by the Company, which embraces Birkenhead (for Liverpool) in the North, to the Scilly Isles in the West; the greater part of Wales as far as Pwllheli in Caernarvonshire; and Inland Districts such as the Malvern Hills, Wye Valley, etc. Many of them have been rewritten and others revised. New slides have been added in many lectures and generally they have been brought up-to-date. Two new lectures have been added recently, viz.: "The Channel Islands" and "The Cotswolds," making a total of twenty-one different lectures available:-

THE UPPER REACHES OF THE THAMES. From Staines to Oxford through the famous Thames Valley	66	Slides
OXFORD. A walk round England's greatest University City; its Colleges, Churches, etc.	80	,,
SHAKESPEARE'S COUNTRY. A picturesque trip through Stratford-upon-Avon, Kenilworth, Warwick, Evesham, Broadway, Leamington Spa, etc.	48	,,
THE WYE VALLEY. A trip through the lovely Wye Valley	52	,,
SOUTH WALES. A tour through the Country of Castles and Gardens of Wales ..	72	,,
NORTH WALES. Through the lovely Dee Valley. A delightful trip from Chester, through Llangollen and Dolgelley, to the beautiful Cambrian Coast ..	66	,,
SEVENTY MILES ALONG THE CAMBRIAN COAST. From Pwllheli to Aberystwyth	75	,,
IN THE FOOTSTEPS OF GEORGE BORROW THROUGH "WILD WALES" ..	75	,,
SOUTHERN IRELAND. Amidst its Lakes and Landscapes, or from Paddington to Killarny and Parknasilla, by Fishguard route	73	,,
WONDERFUL WESSEX. A short account of Wiltshire, Somerset, and Dorset, and the "Hardy" Country	69	,,
DEVON: THE SHIRE OF THE SEA KINGS. A delightful journey through North and South Devon	75	,,
THE LORNA DOONE AND WESTWARD HO! COUNTRY. The beauty spots of Somerset and North Devon	74	,,
THE CORNISH RIVIERA. A tour from Paddington to Land's End	72	,,
THE LAND'S END COUNTRY AND THE SCILLIES. Western Cornwall and the Isles of Scilly	75	,,
SOMERSET. A delightful tour through a beautiful County	75	,,
HISTORIC ABBEYS AND CATHEDRALS. Forty Abbeys and Cathedrals in England and Wales on the G.W.R.	67	,,
LEGENDLAND ON THE G.W.R.	100	,,
THE CHANNEL ISLANDS. A tour of fascinating interest through Guernsey, Jersey, Sark, etc.	68	,,
GUERNSEY. The Island of Sunshine. Including Sark, Herm and Alderney	78	,,
THE MALVERN HILLS AND COTSWOLD COUNTRY. A holiday country of infinite variety	75	,,
BATH. England's Premier Spa.	100	,,

The slides are lent free of charge with the exception of any expense which may be incurred outside the usual delivery area. Lecture notes accompany the slides.

It is desirable that **at least two weeks' notice** should be given to the Superintendent of the Line, G.W.R. Paddington Station, London, W.2, for any set of slides required, and **prompt return after use is essential to other bookings being met**. A label for this purpose is enclosed with each box of slides.

Acceptance of the slides will be taken as a guarantee of careful handling.

APPENDIX 4

Check List of Official Postcards

Pictorial Post Cards. Published by the Great Western Railway Co. of some of the beautiful Places and Objects of Interest on the System.

Two for One Penny.

On sale at the Stations and Bookstalls.

Collectors can obtain complete sets 25 for 1/-

The cards between 1898 and 1901 were produced by The Picture Postcard Company comprising of London views and a smaller vignette card. Then in March 1904 the GWR issued the Raphael Tuck series, which was later than other railway companies' issues. From 1904 until the 1922 grouping, a further 250-plus cards were issued, both in sets, series and singles. Other cards were also issued, mainly supplied by Wyndhams. This list is by no means complete but it a useful guide to the cards issued.

LONDON VIEWS by The Picture Postcard Co Ltd. Size 130×85 c1898

Albert Memorial, Kensington Gardens
Bank of England (Vignette)
Cheapside. Looking West (Vignette)
Houses of Parliament, Westminster (Vignette)
Mansion House
Tower Bridge (Vignette)
Trafalgar Square (Vignette)
Trafalgar Square & National Gallery (Vignette)
Westminster Abbey (Vignette)

GENERAL CARDS by The Picture Postcard Co Ltd. Size 130×80 c 1899

Barnstaple	Cardiff. The Gardens, Penarth
Lynmouth	Carmarthen (Carmarthen Junc). Coracle Men
Bath. The Abbey	Cheltenham. The Promenade
Bath. Grand Pump Room	Cheltenham. Pittville Gardens
Bath. The Lower Avon	Clevedon. Clevedon
Bath. Roman Baths	Clevedon. Lady Bay
Birmingham. New Street	Dartmouth. The College
Birmingham. Town Hall	Dartmouth. The Castle
Birmingham. Law Courts	Dartmouth. "The Britannia"
Birmingham. Council House	Dartmouth. "The Discovery"

Dawlish. Dawlish
Devonport. Devonport
Devonport. Cremill Point, Devonport
Dolgelly. Torrent Walk
Dolgelly. Dolgelly and Cader Idris
Exeter. Exeter Cathedral
Exeter. The Nave, Exeter Cathedral
Exeter. The Guildhall, Exeter
Gloucester. The Cathedral
Gloucester. Cathedral Nave
Gloucester. The New Inn
Great Malvern, Swan Pool
Great Malvern, The Abbey Gate
Henley-on-Thames. Henley-on-Thames
Henley-on-Thames. The Regatta
Leamington. The Crescent
Leamington. In the Gardens
Llangollen. The Bridge
Llangollen. Horse Shoe Falls
Llangollen. Vale Crucis Abbey
Maidenhead. Clivedon Woods
Maidenhead. Clivedon Reach
Minehead. Minehead
Minehead. Dunster Castle
Newquay. On the Beach
Newquay. Bedruthan Steps
Oswestry. The Cross
Oxford. Oriel Quadrangle
Oxford. The Isis
Oxford. Magdalen College and Bridge
Oxford. Exeter College Gardens
Oxford. View from Magdalen Tower

Oxford. St. John's College
Penzance. Lands End
Penzance. St. Michael's Mount
Penzance. Lizard Head
Penzance. St. Mary's, Scilly Isles
Plymouth. Eddystone Lighthouse
Plymouth. The Pier, Plymouth
St. Ives. St. Ives
Salisbury. Salisbury Cathedral
Southampton. Western Shore
Stratford-on-Avon. Memorial Theatre
Stratford-on-Avon. Ann Hathaway's
    Cottage
Stratford-on-Avon. Shakespeare's House
Stratford-on-Avon. Holy Trinity Church
Swansea. Mumbles Head and Lighthouse
Teignmouth. Teignmouth
Tenby. Tenby
Tintern. The Abbey
Torquay. Torquay
Torquay. Coast View near Torquay
Truro. The Cathedral (Interior)
Warwick. Warwick Castle
Warwick. Guy's Cliff House
Warwick. Guy's Cliff Mill
Warwick. Kenilworth Castle
Weston-Super-Mare. The Sands
Weymouth. The Harbour, Eventide
Winchester. Winchester Cathedral
Windsor. Windsor Castle
Windsor. East Terrace, Windsor Castle

The next issues of postcards were not until 1904 when Series 1 (25 cards) was launched just ahead of the LNWR's first successful sets. This set was advertised in the January 1904 issue of the *GWR Magazine*.

SERIES No. 1 & 2

Series No. 1 — March 1904. Set of 25 cards printed by R. Tuck and Sons portraying views of 'Western' Territory. Sold from automatic machines at two cards for 1d (unstamped) and one card (stamped)

 1   Weymouth and the Landing Stage
 2   Great Western Express Passenger Engine "City of Bath"
 3   Royal Waiting Room Paddington
 4   Departure Platforms, Paddington Station Hotel
 5   Great Western, Paddington
 6   Early Great Western Broad Gauge Engine "Vulcan"
 7   Latest Type Great Western Engine (No. 98)
 8   Temple Meads Railway Station Bristol
 9   Entrance to Great Western Tunnel, Twerton, Bath
10   How Our Forefathers Travelled in the "Forties"
11   "Up the River" Henley-on-Thames
12   The Vale of Llangollen
13   Great Western Railway Bridge, Maidenhead
14   The Great Western Royal Train
15   Windsor Castle
16   Great Western Railway Bridge, Saltash built 1859
17   Great Western Viaduct Ivybridge, Plymouth
18   Beautiful Berwyn
19   A Famous Great Western Broad Gauge Engine "North Star"
20   A Charming Great Western Hotel, Tregenna Castle, St. Ives
21   One of the Great Western Railway, Channel Islands Fleet
22   Great Western Railway Bridge over the Severn, Arley
23   Great Western Viaduct, Pontcysyllte near Ruabon
24   The Lion Rock, Cheddar
25   An Old Cornish Railway Viaduct, Trenance, St. Austell

These were issued in four different printings including sepia, blue, grey and 'Series 1' being printed on the address side.
Size 140×90
Several changes were noted on the last printing (ie Series 1) of individual cards.

SERIES 2 – October 1904. 25 further sepia cards in this series, again
printed by R. Tuck, size 140×90 'Series 2' printed on address side.

26 Pittville Lake, Cheltenham. Great Western Railway
27 Oxford. Great Western Railway
28 Magdalen Tower Oxford. Great Western Railway
29 On the Way to Mumbles Head from Swansea
30 Warwick Castle. Great Western Railway
31 Old Mill Guy's Cliff near Warwick. Great Western Railway
32 Tree used as Booking Office. Moreton-on-Lugg. Great Western
   Railway
33 Pandy Mill near Dolgelly. Great Western Railway
34 The Lake at Bala. Great Western Railway
35 Shrewsbury. Great Western Railway
36 Exterior Paddington (GWR) Station 1838
37 Interior Paddington (GWR) Station 1854
38 Slough (GWR) Station 1845
39 Quadrangle Eton College. Windsor & Eton (GWR) Station
40 Playing Fields. Eton, Windsor & Eton (GWR) Station
41 On the Way to Beaconsfield by GWR Motor Car
42 Oak Growing Out of a Beech. Burnham Beeches by GWR Motor
   Car from Slough
43 Broad Gauge Engine (GWR) Lord of the Isles
44 Latest Type Passenger Engine (GWR) **Albion** (No. 171)
45 Compound Engine **La France** Constructed in France for the Great
   Western Railway (No. 102)
46 Swindon (GWR) in 1847
47 Bath City. Great Western Railway
48 Great Western Railway. Map of the Cornish Riviera
49 Penzance (GWR) Station and Harbour
50 The Gorge near Cheddar. Great Western Railway

The GWR Magazine of April 1905 reviewed these cards by saying: 'A
decided note of novelty has been struck in selecting the subject for the
third series of picture postcards. This is the reproduction in miniature of
some of the most attractive pictorial posters. Designed by capable artists,
many of the posters have already been much admired by the public, and
their charm is none the less in the form in which they are now produced.
Well lithographed by Messrs Andrew Reid & Co of Newcastle-on-Tyne,
these postcards will doubtless be much sought by collectors'.

SERIES 3 — March 1905. 12 further cards depicting coloured posters.
Sold for 6d the twelve. Size 140×90. Lettered 'G.W.Series 3' on the
picture side.

51 Cornish Riviera—An Ideal Health and Pleasure Resort
52 Blarney Castle. Paddington and Waterford in 13 Hrs.
53 To the Lizard. By Rail and Motor in 8 Hours

54   Lands End. By Rail and Motor Hours from Paddington
55   Dining Cars to Bristol, Exeter, Torquay, Plymouth, Penzance, Newport, Cardiff
56   North Wales. Free Fishing in Bala Lake
57   Xmas Excursions
58   Mounts Bay by Night
59   Week-End Tickets. All the Year Round
60   Picturesque Wales. Tourist Tickets
61   Direct Route to Weymouth
62   To the Upper Thames. Cheap Daily Tickets

SERIES 4 – September 1905. 25 further cards printed in gravure, lettered 'G.W.Series 4' with crest, in left top corner of address side. Size 140×90.

63   Perivale Church. Great Western Railway, Perivale Halt
64   Clievedon Woods. By G.W.R. to Maidenhead
65   Reading from Caversham. Great Western Railway
66   Christchurch, Oxford. Great Western Railway
67   Stratford-on-Avon. Nearest Station, Great Western Railway, Stratford
68   Worcester Cathedral. By Great Western Railway
69   Leamington. Great Western Railway
70   Horse Shoe Falls by Great Western Railway to Berwyn
71   Valle Crucis Abbey, by Great Western Railway to Berwyn
72   Wells Cathedral by Great Western Railway
73   Footbridge to Old Mill by GWR to Cynwydd
74   The Lower Avon, Bath. Great Western Railway
75   Oystermouth Bay. By Great Western Railway to Swansea
76   Bristol Cathedral and College Green. Great Western Railway
77   Minehead. Great Western Railway
78   The Beach, Teignmouth. Great Western Railway
79   Dawlish. Great Western Railway
80   The Cornish Riviera Express near Dawlish. Great Western Railway
81   Paignton. Great Western Railway
82   Dartmouth and Kingswear Castles. Nearest Station GWR Kingswear
83   Fowey (Cornish Riviera) Great Western Railway
84   Truro Cathedral and River Fal. Great Western Railway
85   Newlyn Harbour. Nearest Station GWR Penzance
86   Hugh Town, St. Mary's, Scilly. By Great Western Railway to Penzance
87   Great Western Railway Express Engine (County of Devon No. 3478)

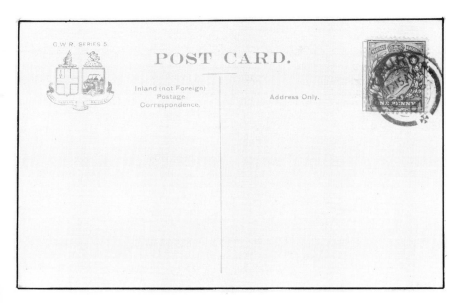

The front and back view of a Great Western Postcard Series 5

SERIES 5 — October 1905. 25 cards in full colour selling for a 1/- the set. Size 140×90. Address side printed in brown with the lettering 'GWR Series 5' (see illustration page 191).

The **Cornishman** near Box
The Beach, Aberystwyth,
  via Great Western Railway
On the Tryweryn, Bala
A Fishpond, Burnham Beeches
On the Wye, Chepstow
Suspension Bridge, Clifton
Upper Falls, Dolgelley
Torr Steps, Dulverton
Old Yarn Market, Conegar
  Tower, Dunster
The Cathedral, Exeter
Glastonbury Abbey. By GWR
  to Wells
The Harbour, Ilfracombe

Lynmouth. By GWR via Barnstaple
St Michael's Mount, Marazion
The River and Church, Marlow
College Barges on the Thames,
  Oxford
The Hoe Promenade, Plymouth
Memorial Theatre,
  Stratford-on-Avon
The Sands, Tenby
The Abbey, Tintern
Cockington Forge, Torquay
Torquay from Rock Walk
Weston-Super-Mare
The Esplanade, Weymouth
Windsor Castle

SERIES 6 — July 1908. 12 cards of locomotive subjects, lettered with the words 'SERIES 6' with scroll. Size 140×90.

3.30pm Express from Paddington Engine No. 178 **Kirkland**
'City' Class. **City of Bath** (No. 3433)
Atlantic Type "Scott" Class **Ivanhoe** (No. 181)
"Star" Class **Evening Star** (No. 4002)
Glehn Compound **La France** (No. 102)
Old Broad Gauge "Single" Wheel **Bulkeley**
"Single" Wheel **Achilles** (No. 3031)
Six-Coupled Bogie Passenger Engine **Viscount Churchill** (No. 175)
"County" Class **County of Radnor** (No. 3818)
Glehn Compound Engine (No. 104)
"Consolidation" Goods Engine (No. 2803)
Double-End Tank Engine (No. 3120)

SERIES 7 — July 1908. 12 cards in colour selling for 6d per set depicting 'The Cornish Riviera'. 'GWR SERIES 7. The Cornish Riviera' printed down the left hand side. Size 140×90.

The Hoe, Plymouth
St. Ives Bay & Porthminster Beach
Royal Albert Bridge, Saltash
  (from Saltash)
Falmouth
The Parade, Penzance
The Sands, Newquay

Mousehole, Penzance
Poldhu Marconi Station
Looe, Mouth of River
Fowey
The Palm Walk, Tresco (V)
Lands End

SERIES 8 —¦ January 1910. 24 cards printed in sepia, selling at 6d for the whole set. Featured in the February 1910 issue of *GWR Magazine*. Printed 'GW SERIES 8 No. then title' on the address side with 'Fishguard Harbour, Port of Call' down the left hand side. Size 140×90.

1   GWR **Cunard Ocean Express** Fishguard-London 261 miles, 4¾ hours
2   Dining Saloon. "Ocean Express"
3   RMS "Lusitania" sighted approaching Fishguard
4   RMS "Mauretania"
5   RMS "Mauretania" entering Fishguard Harbour
6   RMS "Lusitania" approaching Fishguard
7   Passenger Tender approaching RMS "Mauretania" Fishguard Harbour
8   RMS "Mauretania" at Anchor, Fishguard Harbour
9   RMS "Lusitania" at Anchor, Fishguard Harbour
10   RMS "Mauretania" at Fishguard Harbour
11   GWR Passenger Tender approaching Quay, Fishguard Harbour Station
12   RMS "Mauretania" at Anchor, Fishguard Harbour
13   GWR Tender Transferring Passengers, Fishguard Harbour
14   Passengers Transferring to Tender, Fishguard Harbour
15   Passengers Transferring to Tender, Fishguard Harbour
16   Tender Transferring Mails, Fishguard Harbour
17   G.W.R. Mail Tender
18   Passenger Tender leaving RMS "Mauretania"
19   RMS "Mauretania" in Fishguard Harbour
20   Passengers landing at Fishguard Harbour Station
21   Passengers landing at Fishguard Harbour
22   Welsh Girls in National Costume at Fishguard
23   Landing Mails, Fishguard Harbour Station
24   GWR "Ocean Express" leaving Fishguard

SERIES 9 — No date of issue. 12 cards labelled 'SERIES 9'. Size 140×90.

Bradley Woods, Newton Abbot
Brixham—The Harbour
Dawlish from Lea Mount
Ilfracombe (Harbour)
Ivybridge—The Bridge
Kingswear Castle
Castle Rock, Lynton (via Barnstaple, Great Western Rly)
Plymouth—The Sound & Drake's Island
Salcombe—North Sands & Bolt Head (via Kingsbridge, Great Western Railway)
Teignmouth
The East Lyn & Lynton (via Barnstaple & Great Western Rly)
Torquay from Rock Walk

SERIES 10 — 1922 issued. 8 cards in sepia printing. Address side printed in brown with wording 'Published by the Great Western Railway' on the left side. Size 140×90.

The Lands End	Shakespeare's House, Stratford-on-Avon
Lynmouth	The River Wye (from Symonds Yat)
Pembroke Castle	Torquay (Harbour)
St. Michael's Mount, Penzance	Warwick Castle

SERIES 11 — c 1923. 24 cards depicting Cornish and Devonshire views. Size 140×90.

Clovelly	Cliff Road, Falmouth
Dittisham-on-Dart	Gylyndune Beach, Falmouth
Exeter Cathedral, The Nave	Kynance Cove
Fingle Bridge, Dartmoor	Lands End
Ilfracombe from Hillsboro	Looe
Lynmouth	Morrab Gardens, Penzance
North Sands and Bolt Head, Salcombe	Newquay, Tolcarne Beach
Pier and Mt. Edgecumbe, Plymouth	Polperro
Teignmouth, Sea Front	Polrunn from Fowey Harbour
The Harbour, Brixham	Porthminster Beach, St. Ives
The Sands, Dawlish	St. Ives, Carbis Bay
Torquay	Truro Cathedral

SERIES 12 — c 1924. 20 cards issued with the publication **Cathedrals**. Each card carried a lengthy description and several were overprinted to advertise the book, 18 listed here with two titles unknown.

Birmingham Cathedral
Gloucester Cathedral
Gloucester Cathedral, Doorway
Gloucester Cathedral, Cloisters
Gloucester Cathedral, Choir
Hereford Cathedral, 12th Century Font
Hereford Cathedral, The Chained Library
Hereford Cathedral, Tomb of Thomas of Hereford
St. David's Cathedral, Bishop's Palace Ruins
St. David's Cathedral, Choir
St. David's Cathedral, Rose Window
St. David's Cathedral, Roof of Lantern Tower
St. David's Cathedral, Ruins of St. Mary's Chapel
St. David's Cathedral, Exterior from N.E.
St. David's Cathedral, St. David's Casket
St. David's Cathedral, St. David's Altar
Worcester Cathedral, Choir
Worcester Cathedral, Cloisters

Further Cathedral cards were issued after Series 12, some are listed here.

Birmingham Cathedral, The Choir
The Nave, Bath Abbey
Brecon Cathedral, Choir and Nave
Bristol Cathedral, The Nave
Chester Cathedral, Choir
Chester Cathedral from S.E.
Watching Chamber of the Shrine of St. Frideswide,
Oxford, Christ Church Chapel
Exeter Cathedral (exterior view)
Exeter Cathedral, The Nave
Hereford Cathedral (exterior view)
Llandaff Cathedral, The Choir
Llandaff Cathedral, West Front
St. Mary Redcliffe, Bristol, North Aisle
St. Mary Radcliffe, Bristol (exterior view)
St. Pauls Cathedral, The Choir
Salisbury Cathedral
Salisbury Cathedral, Choir and Nave
Southwark Cathedral, The Nave
Southwark Cathedral, Exterior from London Bridge
Truro Cathedral
Truro Cathedral, Reredos
The Nave, Wells Cathedral
Wells Cathedral, West Front
Westminster Abbey from the South West
Westminster Abbey, Unknown Warrior's Tomb
The Reredos, Winchester Cathedral
Winchester Cathedral, West Front
Worcester Cathedral (exterior view)

Other cards issued are as follows:

Issued 1908. 4 cards in green. Fishguard Routes.
Issued 1915/16. 5 cards (one in green, 4 in red), Continental
Ambulance Train.
Issued 1922/24. 12 cards. Dock Views.
Issued 1904. 15 cards. Correspondence Cards. Depicting resorts, 4
issues in different colours.
Issued 1912. Over 200 cards issued in the CORRESPONDENCE series
of cards. A large issue in four different printing colours for the
photographs and red printing on the address side. This series was known
as the Wyndham Series and depicted scenes around the region of the
GWR. This was by far the greater number of picture postcards ever
issued by any company for correspondence purposes, and from records,
no railway scenes were used.

Issued 1913/1915. 16 cards. CORRESPONDENCE CARDS (3rd issue). Printed in 3 colours, (green, brown & grey). Address side printed in green. This series can be identified by printing reference numbers in the top left hand corner.

Issued 1905-1909. 3 cards DINING CAR SERIES. Differed from above by company two-shielded crest and the word DINING CAR.

Issued 1900-1915. 16 cards RESTAURANT CARS. Printed in grey or brown with the address side printed in brown. The two shielded crest with wording 'GWR EXPRESS TRAIN en route. RESTAURANT CAR .... 19......'

Issued December 1909. 3 cards depicting Engravings for correspondence cards. Used to advertise the large Fine Art Engravings of 8"×6".

Issued c 1900-1924. 8 cards known of Locomotives. Size 140×90.

General notes about lesser issues by the G.W.R.

Cards were issued in postcard size for SEAT RESERVATION, POSTERS, IRISH ROUTES, RESTAURANT CAR MAPS, HEALTH, SUNNY FALMOUTH, TORQUAY PAGEANT, HOTEL CARDS (various GWR Hotel issues) CORNISH RIVIERA, HOLIDAY HAUNTS, FOOTBALL, ARTIST'S OF GWR and REGISTRATION CARDS.

This listing is nowhere complete and has been compiled by Picton Publishing from the *GWR Magazine*, GWR Records of the Printing Dept and various books on the subject.

There are numerous single photographic and coloured views which exist even with the company's credits on them but are not listed in official records and there could be varieties of the cards listed but this appendix does give some idea of the enormous effort the Printing Department put into the PICTURE POSTCARD. (The GWR's cheapest image of publicity!)

POSTCRIPT

A chapter on publicity is included in *The Great Western Railway: 150 Glorious Years* by Patrick Whitehouse and David St John Thomas, Newton Abbot, 1984.

Acknowledgements

Collecting the material for this book has been a voyage of discovery. In my business as a bookseller I had known for many years that the Great Western Railway was unusually active in the publication of books, and a decision to make as complete a collection as possible of the company's publications led me, almost inevitably, to search out other forms of publicity matter. By the time I had worked through sixty years of *Great Western Railway Magazine* I began to appreciate the immense scope of the company's publicity. The pity is that I commenced gathering this material many years too late, for so much is now irretrievably lost. The compilation of the check lists of publications and jig-saw puzzles has been hampered by the difficulty in locating some of the material, which will, I hope, be sufficient justification for any omissions.

As with most railway books, serious research commenced at British Railways Board Archives at 66 Porchester Road—a singularly appropriate place in this case since that building once housed the stationery and printing department of the GWR. My thanks are due to Mr E. Atkinson, the archivist, and his successor, Mr E. H. Fowkes, for allowing me to examine the material in their care and to use the periodicals in the record office library.

It soon became apparent, however, that I should have to go farther afield, for though Great Western publicity matter housed at Porchester Road far exceeds that of any other company in quantity, it still represents only a small part of the total, and some years of hunting were necessary before I had accumulated sufficient material for even the present brief survey.

But it is one thing to gather a collection of books, folders and handbills, and quite another to discover what went on behind the scenes to produce them. My quest for the background to Great Western publicity has been immeasurably eased by the help I have received from the Public Relations Department at Paddington, where facilities were provided for me to talk to two former members of the GWR publicity department staff. Of these, Mr Lionel

Kathrens, who is still 'on the Western' in the Public Relations office, has given me every possible help on my frequent visits to Paddington, while Mr Bill Dunham, now retired, has patiently listened to my many problems, answered strings of questions, and read the typescript.

I have also received every help from the Photographic Section at Paddington. Prints from their collection, and illustrations of post-1919 material, still in copyright, are reproduced by kind permission of the Public Relations Officer, British Railways Western Region.

I am also indebted to Miss Maxwell Fraser, who gave me much valuable information about the department for which she wrote so much, and about her father, W. H. Fraser, its one-time head.

I also owe thanks to Mr Charles Mayo for help with the chapter on pictorial posters, with which he was so intimately connected, and to Mr Donald Saunders of British Transport Films for information on Great Western films.

Among the many other people who have helped me I must mention Mr O. P. Chandler of The Chad Valley Co Ltd, Mr Michael Harris, Mr Malcolm Guest, Mr Trefor David, Mr David Lyall and Mr John Strange. The section on picture post-cards owes much to Mr Geoffrey Green, and Mr David Hyde kindly allowed me to photograph his copy of the poster which forms the frontispiece.

I wish also to acknowledge help from Miss D. M. Norris and Miss D McCulla, of the Local Studies section of Birmingham Reference Library, Mr Paul Morgan and the staff of the John Johnson Collection, Bodleian Library, and Miss P. Y. Lewis, librarian of Gloucestershire College of Art and Design.

The late Mr George Dyall sent me a sheet of notes very shortly before he died. Had I been able to glean more from his memories of the publicity department, which he joined in 1897, this would have been a better book. As it is, I claim for it no more than that it is a gathering together of scattered material on a sadly neglected subject. I hope a better pen than mine will one day build on these modest foundations.

R.B.W.

1969

Notes on Sources

The records and files of the Great Western Railway publicity department are now lost, and information has had to be obtained from widely scattered sources, of which the most important are given below. The memories of the few surviving members of the department's staff have been invaluable, and their help is acknowledged on page 187.

British Railways Board Archives
Class reference GW 19. A good, but by no means complete, collection of sale publications, some other booklets and folders, and a set of *Holiday Haunts*.
Class reference GW 18 contains several special reports on advertising. Bound sets of railway periodicals, notably the *Railway Magazine, Railway Gazette, Railway News* and *Railway Times*, a complete set of the *Great Western Railway Magazine*, and the house journals of other railway companies.
British Railways (Western Region) Public Relations Department. A collection of photographs of pictorial posters, 1898-1947.
Bodleian Library, Oxford. The John Johnson Collection contains a mass of railway printed matter of all kinds, although Great Western publicity is not particularly well represented.
Newspaper files are available in most of the larger reference libraries, and at the British Museum newspaper section at Colindale.

By far the most important source, especially for organisation and staff matters, and for information on the minor aspects of publicity covered in Chapter 6, is the *Great Western Railway Magazine* (November 1888-December 1947). There is hardly a single issue that does not contain some reference to publicity. The principal articles dealing specifically with the subject are:

May 1907	Coloured plate of early pictorial posters
July 1908	Coloured and monochrome plates of pictorial posters
Aug 1910	Page 201. Illustration of posters and press announcements
Sep 1911	Page 247. Illustration of posters, folders etc
Apr 1913	Pages 102-3. 'Candidus': 'Do Railways believe in advertising?'
Feb 1914	Pages 45-6. A. H. Edwards: Railway-Map Making by Wax Plate Process
July 1914	Pages 185-6. The 'Story of the Holiday Line' told by Living Pictures
May 1915	Page 118. The South Western Railway Magazine
Mar 1930	Pages 101-4. Maxwell Fraser: 'The Production of "Holiday Haunts"'
Feb 1931	Pages 71-4, and Mar 1931, pages 113-16. W. H. Jarvis: 'A Decade of Progress in Great Western Typography'
Apr 1931	Pages 173-5. C. S. Lock: 'How the First British Train "Talkie" was made'
Aug 1931	Pages 343-6. C. S. Lock: 'The Gainsborough Ghost Train Goes Great Western'
Sep 1931	Pages 391-4. [E. S. Hadley]: 'Some Less Familiar Industries in Great Western Territory. No 2. The Chad Valley Works'
Oct 1932	Pages 379-80. W. G. C[hapman]: 'The G.W.R. Central Information Bureau'
Mar 1933	Pages 114-17. W. H. Jarvis: 'The Great Western Railway Guide, "Holiday Haunts"'
Nov 1934	Page 520. G. E. Orton: 'A General Review of Railway Publicity'
May 1935	Pages 262-3. 'Making a G.W.R. Centenary Film'

Sep 1935 Page 453. G. H.: 'The Great Western Railway Centenary Film'

Oct 1935 Pages 547-54. 'The Great Western Railway Company's Centenary Celebrations'

Aug 1936 Pages 408-9. ' "Loco's of the 'Royal Road' " '

June 1938 Pages 235-6. W. G. Chapman: 'The G.W.R. at Your Service. The Work of the Enquiry Bureau'

Nov 1944 Pages 170-1. 'Training the Paddington "Trains Trust" '

Holiday Haunts (1906-16, 1921-40, 1947) contains more of historical interest than is generally realised. There are also very useful lists of publications, lantern lectures and jig-saw puzzles.

Great Western Railway (London) Lecture and Debating Society. A much-neglected source of information on a wide range of topics. Two papers on publicity are:

Session 1924-5, No 179. D. Richards: 'Advertising with special reference to railway publicity'. 20 pages.

Session 1934-5, No 284. G. E. Orton: 'Railway Publicity'. 16 pages.

The following books have supplied additional information and background:

Behrend, G. *Gone with Regret*. Lambarde Press 1964

Christiansen, R. and R. W. Miller. *The Cambrian Railways,* David & Charles, 2 vols, 1967-[8]

Harris, M. *Great Western Coaches 1890-1954.* David & Charles 1966

Hutchison, H. F. *The Poster*. Studio-Vista, 1968

Jones, S. R. *Posters and Publicity*. The Studio, 1926

Jones, S. R. *Posters and their Designers*. The Studio, 1924

Lewis, J. *Printed Ephemera*. Faber & Faber, for W. S. Cowell Ltd, 1962

MacDermot, E. T. *History of the Great Western Railway.* G.W.R., 2 vols in 3, 1927-31, and second edition, edited C. R. Clinker, Ian Allan, 2 vols 1964

Mercer, F. A. & W. Gaunt. *Posters & Publicity*. The Studio, 1928

Nock, O. S. *The Great Western Railway in the 19th Century.* Ian Allan 1962

Nock, O. S. *The Great Western Railway in the 20th Century,* Ian Allan 1964

Ottley, G. *A Bibliography of British Railway History.* Allen & Unwin, 1965

Pole, [Sir] F. J. C. *Felix J. C. Pole His Book.* Privately Printed, 1954, reprinted 1969

Sparrow, W. Shaw. *Advertising and British Art.* Bodley Head 1924

Staff, F. *The Picture Postcard & Its Origin.* Lutterworth Press 1966

Turner, E. S. *The Shocking History of Advertising!*

Index

Illustrations are shown in *italic*, main references in **bold** type

Abbeys, 30, **93**, 101, 152
Advertising, *see* Publicity
Advertising agents, 19, 42, 43, 84, 113
Advertising inspectors, 10, 113, 136
Agencies, GWR, 152
Agricultural shows, 26, 80, **149**
Air services, 14, 46, 82, 120
Aldin, Cecil, 65
Aldington, C. E., 68, 166
Allen, T. I., 22, 37
Ancillary services, 76, 77, 80
Anrooy, Avan, *36*, 74
Artists, commissioning of, 69, 70; *see also under artists' names*
Associated British & Irish Railways (ABIR), 34, 38, 82

Badminton line, 106
Baltimore & Ohio Railroad, *54*, 133
Barman, Christian, 38-9, 102
Bath & West Show, 149, 150
Beasley, Ammon, 162
Beaumont, C., 38, 169
Beautiful Brittany, 86
Beer, G. E., 91
Beggarstaffs, the, 65
Bills, *see* handbills, posters
Biograph Company, The, 124
Birmingham, train services to, *53*, 151, 155; posters, *35*, 67; in *Holiday Haunts*, 111, 113

Booklets & folders, 26, 30, 47, *53*, *54*, 77, 79, **77-82**, 93, 94, *94*, *103*, 160; distribution of, 78, 80, 81, 82, 95; production & printing of, 81
Book markers, *90*, 154-5
Books, book publishing, *see* Sale publications
Bourne, J. C., 16
Bradley, A. G., 99
Bradshaw's *Guide*, 154
Brangwyn, Frank, 69
Bristol & Exeter Rly, 48, 157
British Empire Exhibition, 32, 131-3, 136, 137
British Railways, Western Region, 40, 102, 122, 169
Brittany, *18*, 67, 86
Broadcasting, 150
Broadley, A. M., 84, 86, 95, 96, 98, 112
Brown, Gregory, 69
Brown, P. Irwin, 74
Buckle, Claude, 74
Burlinson, N. J., 22
Burrow, Ed J. & Co Ltd, 95-6
Buses, *see* Road motors
Button, H. B., 29
'Buy British' campaign, 27

Caerphilly Castle, 131, 132
Caerphilly Castle (engine), 131, 132, 137; jig-saw, 137, 138

Cambrian Coast, The, 88, 114
Cambrian Rlys, 29, 88
Cambrian Resorts Association, 29
Cameron, Sir D. Y., 70
Campaigns, 27, 28, 34, 42, 45; *see also* Slogans
Camping, *54*, 79, 99
Camping coaches, *54*, 80, 99, 121
Carnivals, 158
Carriage pictures, 111, **142**, *146*
Cassell's *Guide* to GWR, 19
Castles, 30, 93, 152
Cathedrals, 30, *89*, **91-3**, 142, 152
Cathedral Guide Series, 182
Centenary of GWR, **34**, 91, 101, 120, 128; film, 34, **128**; broadcast, 150; poster, *36*, 74, 75
Chad Valley Co Ltd, The, 136, 138, 139, 140
Channel Islands, 66
Chapman, W. G., 30, 87, **88**, **91**, 155
Cheap trips, *see* Excursions
Cheltenham Flyer, 88, 91, *92*, 120
Cheltenham Flyer, jig-saw, *108*, 139; coloured plate, 139, luggage label, *143*, 153
Cheltenham—Honeybourne line, 104
Chéret, Jules, 65
Chilterns, the, 151
Clinker, C. R., 96
Coloured plates, 139
'Come to Britain' campaign, 27, 34
Commercial advertising dept, 31, 32
Competitions, 69, **147-8**, 167
Continent, advertising on the, 45, 78
Cook, Thos, & Son Ltd, 24, 152
Cornish Riviera, *see* Devon & Cornwall
Cornish Riviera, The [Broadley], 25, **83**, **84**, *85*, 104, 124, 148
Cornish Riviera, The (Mais), *72*, **98**, 101, 115, 120
'Cornish Riviera Express', 104, 105, 129, **147**; luggage label, *143*
Cornwall Rly, 48
Coronation, 1937, 34, 37, *54*, 121
Cotswolds, *53*, 79
Cross-country services, 78, 109, 113, 155

Daily Mail, 43, 91, 147
Davis, F. R. E., 39, 150

Devon, *72*, 84, 86
Devon & Cornwall, 24, 30, 43, 45, *53*, 73, 106, 135, 147; films, 124, 128; exhibitions, 134; jig-saws, 137; postcards, 141; *see also* Devon, Glorious Devon, Cornish Riviera, Posters
Dewar, Major M. J. M., **32**, 37, 38, 40
Diesel rail car, 135, 137
Dining cars, *35*, 111, 153
Directories, 46
Docks, 132, 135
Dunkirk and the Great Western, 102
Dyall, George, 37

'Earlier Holidays' campaign, 27, 34, 43
Edwards, Archibald, 24
Emlyn, Viscount (later Earl Cawdor), 22
Engine names & numbers, books on, *71*, **86**, **87**
Enquiry Bureau, Central, 91, **155-7**
Enquiry offices, temporary, 26, 133, 134, **148-50**
Excursions & cheap trips, 15, *15*, *17*, *20*, 24, 42, 43, 45, 48, *55*, *56*, *57*, *58*, *60*, *61*, *63*, *64*, 75, 155
Excursion Arrangements, *17*, 24, **47**, **48**, *61*
Exhibitions, 26, 37, **129-35**; Great (1851), 129, 130; British Empire (1924-5), 32, **131-3**, 136, 137

'Fair Deal for the Railways' campaign, 28
Films, 34, 37, **124**, **127-9**; Centenary, 34, **128**
Fishguard, 67, 78, 86, 104, 106, 124, 130, 141, 142
Folders, *see* Booklets & Folders
'For Boys of all Ages' series, 30, *71*, **88**, **91**, *92*, 101, *103*, 131, 142
Fraser, Alec, 66, 67
Fraser, Maxwell, 46, 79, 82, **101**, 102, **116**, 121
Fraser, W. H., 25, **29**, **30**, **31**, 37, 38, 68, 70, 99, 101, 115
Free Booklets, 182

Gainsborough Pictures Ltd, 127
George, Dorothee, 67
Gill, Eric, 49

Glorious Devon, **98**, 101, 115, 120
Goble, Warwick, 74, 81
'Go Great Western' slogan, 27, *27,*
28, 114, 155, 157, 158
Goods services, 45, *53*, 76, 77, 80,
82, 120, 149; at exhibitions, 134;
maps, 159, 160
Grand, K. W. C., **31**, 32, 38, 101
Great Bear, The (engine), 131, 132
Great Exhibition, 1851, 129, 130
Great Western Magazine, The
(1862-4), 161-3
GWR Coffee Tavern Co Ltd, 165
GWR-GC Joint line, 86, 106
Great Western Railway Magazine,
87, 88, 102, 138, *144*, **161-70**;
advertising & sale of, 111, 164,
165, 166, 167; art edition, 165;
competitions in, 69, 148, 167;
contents, 164, 165, 166; editors,
see next entry; first issue, 163;
format, 166, 168, 169; insurance
edition, 168; 'Is it safe?' campaign, 167; price, 164, 168; sale
of plates from, 139, 164; taken
over by GWR Co, 165
Great Western Railway Magazine,
editors, C. Beaumont, 38, 169;
E. S. Hadley, **166**, **167**, 168; F. J.
C. Pole, 28, 96, **165**, **166**, 167; J.
K. Skellern, 164; R. F. Thurtle,
168, 169; W. H. M. Woodley,
169
GWR Operatic Societies, 128
GWR Social & Educational Union,
157, 167
GWR Staff Superannuation & Guarantee Funds, 162
GWR Temperance Union, 130, **163**,
165
Grierson, James, 21, 22
Grouping, 28, 29, 37, 48, 68, 88,
114, 159
Guide books, advertisements in,
16, 19, *20*, 46
Guide books to GWR, 16, *21*, *23*

Hadley, E. S., **166-7**, 168
Handbills, 22, 24, 26, 41, 45, **47**,
50, *55*, *58-9*, *60*, 81; layout &
printing of, 19, 21, 22, **47**, 114
'Handy Aids' series, *93*, 93-5
Hassall, John, 65, 66
Haunts and Hints for Anglers, 86

Helping Hand Fund, 167
Hiking, 79, *79*, 99
Hill, Walter, 24, 105
*Historic Sites and Scenes of Eng-
land*, 84
History of the GWR, 86, **96**
*History of the Great Western Rail-
way* (MacDermot), 96
Holiday Guides, 16, 24, 103, 105
Holiday Haunts, *14*, 25, 37, *90*, 99,
104-21, *117*, *119*, 139, 148, 159;
advertisements in, 42, 98, 101,
102, 106, 109, *110*, 111, 120, 138,
142, 145; *146*; advertising of, 43,
58, 68, 103, 112, *120*, 134, 152;
editing & production of, 38, 101,
112, 115, 116, 118, 121; first issue,
1906, 104-5; layout of, **105-6**, 109,
112, 113, 114, 115, 118, 120; printing of, 113, 114, **116**, 118, 121;
sales and distribution of, 30, 34,
112, 115, 116, 118, 120, 134
'Holiday Line' slogan, 24, *24*, *26*,
27, 111, 131; competition, 148
Holiday Season Tickets, 121, 153
Holiday towns and areas, *see*
Resorts
Holiday traffic, 16, 24, 32, 76, 99,
104, 155, 156
Homes for All, 6, 126, 151-2
Hotels, 80, 102, 153; Fishguard
Bay, 67, 106, 142; GW Royal,
143; Manor House, 102, 127,
142, *143*; Tregenna Castle, 102,
142
Hurford, R. F., 37

Inglis, J. C. (later Sir James), 25,
42, 105, 147
International Hotel Alliance, 30
Ireland, 43; posters, 67; books, 84,
86, 101; folder, *53*
'Is Your Journey Really Necessary?' campaign, 76
'It's Quicker by Rail' campaign, 27,
42, 45

James, Dr M. R., 93
Jarvis, W. H., 48, 75, 95
Jig-saw Puzzles, 26, 73, *108*, 120,
132, **136-9**, **Appx 2**; advertising
of, 138, 139; boxes, *125*, 138,
139; sales of, 134, 137, **138**
John, Augustus, 70

Johnston, Edward, 49

Kauffer, E. McKnight, 69, 72, 74, 98
King Edward (engine), 139
King George V (engine), coloured plate, 139; in USA 54, 133; jigsaw, 137, 138; model, 135; postcard, 142

Lampitt, Ronald, 75
Land Cruises, 80, 82, 120
Lantern Lectures, 122, 123, 124, 128, 185 Appendix 3.
Legend Land, 88
Liverpool & Manchester Rly Centenary, 134
Lock, C. S., 38
Loco's of "The Royal Road", 91
London & North Eastern Rly, 49, 65, 69, 70, 74, 131
London & North Western Rly, 68, 141, 142
London, Midland & Scottish Rly, 30, 69, 70, 81, 135
London Passenger Transport Board, 38
London Underground Railways, 49, 69, 98
Lord of the Isles (engine), 130, 132
Luggage labels, 143, 152-3, 153
'Lyonesse' [G. B. Barham], 88
Lyttelton, Lord, 163

MacDermot, E. T., 96
Magazines, railway companies', 99; Gt Central Journal, 164; Gt Eastern Rly Magazine, 164; Gt Northern Journal, 161; Gt Western Magazine (1862-4), 161-3; Gt Western Rly Magazine (1888-1947) see Great Western Railway Magazine; L.N.W.R. Gazette, 164; North Eastern Rly Magazine, 164; South Western Gazette, 164; South Western Magazine, 164
Mais, S. P. B., 30, 98, 115
Manchester & Milford Rly, 86
Maps, 78, 84, 106, 113, 137, 151, 158-60
Mason, Frank, 69
Mayo, C. H. J., frontispiece, 71, 75, 142

Measom, George, 16, 19, 23
Menu cards, 153, 154
Merton Park Studios, 128
Midland Rly, 162
Milford, George, 96
Milne, Sir James, 39, 170
Monograms, GWR, circa 1912, 31, 32; competition for design, 147, 148; roundel, 31, 32, 50, 74, 81, 102, 118, 142, 159
Moore, F., 130, 139
Mott, Ralph, 75, 80, 81, 82

Narrow gauge rlys, 113, 114
Nationalisation, 31, 39, 76, 169
Newbould, Frank, 35, 69, 74, 76, 79, 81, 82
Newspapers, see Press
Next Station, 39, 39, 102
North Star (engine, replica), 54, 132, 133, 134
North Wales, 84
North Warwickshire line, 151, 152

Oman, Sir Chas, 93
Orpen, Sir Wm, 70
Orton, G. E., 32, 38, 41, 51, 80

Page, Hugh E., 99
Painting book, 140
Pendennis Castle (engine), 131, 132
Penny a Mile fares, 45
Petrie, Graham, 73
Photographs, for Holiday Haunts, 116; in carriages, 142, 146
Pick, Frank, 69
Pike, Joseph, 155
Pole, F. J. C. (later Sir Felix), 25, 30, 68, 87; and GWR History, 96; and King George V, 133; and Magazine, 28, 96, 165, 166, 167; and publicity, 28, 48, 68, 69, 91, 101, 136, 139
Postcards, picture, 74, 130, 140; GWR, 107, 111, 140-1; LNWR, 141, 142; sales from slot machines, 142 Appendix 4, 186-196
Posters, 26, 41; chalk, 157, 158; display of, 50, 135, 152; handwritten, 50; value of, 50
Posters, letterpress, 16, 21, 45, 47-50, 52, 56-7, 62-4; display of, 19, 47; layout & printing, 21, 22, 47-50
Posters, pictorial, frontispiece, 16,

17, 18, 27, 30, 37, 38, **65-76**; at temporary enquiry offices, 149, 150; comment on, 67, 68, 70; competition for designs, 69, 148; cost of, 67; distribution of, 67, 76; first GWR, 17, 66; origin of, 65; printing of, 70, 75; reproductions of, 66, 141; sale of, 145; Bath, 73, 74; Birmingham services, 35, 67; Brittany, 67; centenary, 36, 74; Channel Is, 66; Chepstow, 74; Cotswolds, 75; Devon & Cornwall, 18, 35, 66, 67, 68, 73, 74, 75; Exeter cathedral, 73; Holiday Haunts, 112; Hotels, 67; Ireland, 67; Malvern, 73; Oxford, 74; Restaurant cars, 35; Road motors, 66; Saltash bridge, 36, 74; Somerset, 74; Speed to the West, frontispiece, 75; Steamer services, 67; Thames, 67; Wales, 67, 74; Warwick Castle, 73; Windsor Castle, 75

Potter, Frank, 68

Pratt, E. A., 87, 88

Press advertising, 15, 16, 19, 22, 26, 30, **41-7**, 44, 75, 148; comment, 68; editorial articles, 46; foreign, 45; visits, 30

Press Bureau, 46, 169

Press Officer, 38

Printers, 22, 49; Arrowsmith, J. W., 49; Ballantyne Press, 88, 91; Billing, Martin, 49; Brendon, Wm, 113; Burns, G., 161; Butler & Tanner, 114, 118, 121; Carlton Press, 164; Chance & Bland, 49; Chiswick Press, 96; Geographia, 159; Johnston, W. & A. K., 159; Judd & Co, 48; Kelly & Kelly, 88; McCorquodale, 48; Petty & Sons, 81; Philip, Geo, 159; Reid, Andrew, 66, 67; Sun Engraving Co., 121; Vandyck Printers, 114; Walker, Emery, 159; Waterlow & Sons, 48, 113; Wones, Joseph, 49; Wyman & Sons, 48, 113, 114, 159

Publicity, see also Advertising

Publicity Agents and Officers, Dewar, Major M. J. M., 32, 37, 38, 40; Dyall, George (acting), 37; Fraser, W. H., 25, **29**, **30**, 31, 37, 38, 68, 70, 99, 115; Grand,

K. W. C., **31**, 32, 38, 101; Hurford, R. F. (acting), 37; Orton, G. E., **32**, 38, 41, 51, 80

Publicity, cost of, 46, 48, 50, 67, 73, 75

Publicity dept (formerly Advertising dept), becomes publicity dept, 29, 68; enlarged, 29, 68; formation of, 21; transfer to Supt of Line, 22; transfer to Gen Manager, 38

Publicity, joint, 34, 45, 81, 82, 133, 134, 135; ABIR, **34**, 38, 82; with LMS, 30, 81; with municipalities, 67; with resorts, **30**, 73, 81, 112; with SR, 30

Publicity, other rly companies, 22, 49, 69, 70, 83, 103, 120, 141, 152; see also under companies' names

Public relations, 28; chief officer for, 38

Purvis, Tom, 69

Puzzle Trains, 138

Race to the Ocean Coast, 138, **139-40**

Railway Centenary, 1925, 132

Railway Clearing House, 34, 38

Railway Gazette, 148

Railway Magazine, 74, 147

Railway Ribaldry, 33, 34, 101, 150

Railways Act, 1921, see Grouping

Ralph & Mott, 75, 80, 81, 82

Rambles series, 71, 99, 100, 101

Rambling, 79, 79, 99

Receiving offices, 152

Reilly, Michael, 74

Resorts, 30, 78, 79, 98, 105; posters for, 73, 76; maps showing, 160; see also Posters, pictorial; Publicity, joint

Restaurants cars, 111, 153

Road Motors, 17, 26, 53, 66, 109, 111, 124; used for advertising, 26, 107, **135-6**

Road transport, competition from, 16, 27, 30, 76, 104, 120, 134

Robinson, W. Heath, 34, 101, 150

Rural London, 84, 86

Safety Movement, 167

Sale publications, 30, 71-2, 75-6, **83-103**, 89, 92-4, 97, 100, 103, Appx 1; advertisements in, 42, 84, 85, 102, 103; advertising of,

43, 84, *85*, 86, 98, 102, 109, 111, 135, 142; bound editions, 84, 95, 98, Appx 1; production & warehousing, 102; sales of, 84, 88, 92, 98, 101, 102, 136, 149; travel books, 25, 47, *71-2*, 81, *85*, **83-103**, *100*, 159, Appx 1; *for individual books see under titles. See also* Printers, Type faces

Sawyer, Arthur, 31, 81

Sayer, J. P., 74

Scotland, advertising in, 135, 136

Secretan, M., *36*, 74

Shakespeare Express, 153, *153*

Skellern, J. K., 164

Slogans, 24, *24*, 27, *26-8*, 76, 111, 114, 131, 155, 157, 158; *see also* Campaigns

Somerset, 24, *100*, 101, 120

Somerset, 100, 101, 120

South Devon Rly, 48

South Wales, 84, 86

South Wales Rly, 106

Southern Ireland [Broadley], 84, 86

Southern Ireland (Fraser), 101

Southern Railway, 45, 98

Southport Flower Show, 149

Sparrow, W. Shaw, 70

Staff and publicity, 157-8

Stanier, W. A. (later Sir Wm), 133

Station gardens, 157

Station Masters, 50, 51, **112, 113**

Stationery & printing dept, 72, 73, 75, 96, 102, 116, 138, 153, 159, 160; supt, 48, 75, 95

Steamer services, 86; posters, 67; exhibitions, 130, 131, 135

Strand Films, 128

Studio, The, 147

Suburban traffic, 151

Swindon works, guide to, 10, 102, 128, 154; royal visits to, 154

Taff Vale Rly, 162

Taylor, Fred, 69, 73, 137

Teasdale, W. M., 69, 70

10.30 Limited, The, 71, 88, 98, 148

Thames, river, 67, 151

Through the Window series, 78, **95-6**, *97*, 101

Thurtle, R. F., 168, 169

Time book, public, 19, 24, 43, 47, 152, 159, **160**

Times, The, 34, 41, 42, 91

Toulouse-Lautrec, 65

Tourist Arrangements, *see* Excursion Arrangements

Track Topics, 91

Transport Act, 1947, 31, 39, 76, 169

Travel books, *see* Sale Publications

Twickenham Studios, 127

Type-faces, on GWR, 48, 49; Centaur, 99; Cheltenham, 49, 114, 120; De Vinne, 114; Garamond, 98; Gill Sans, 49, 76, 120, 122; Winchester Bold, 48, 49

Type-faces, on LNER, 49; on London Underground Rlys, 49

Tyrrell, G. N., 22

United States, advertising in, 45, 78, 111, 128; and Canada, 31, 32, 78; *King George V* in, *54*, 133

Visits, royal, 154

Wales, 24, 29, 43, *53*, 67, 113, 114; books, 84; Eisteddfod, 149; exhibitions, 135; film, 124; posters, 66, 67

Walker, Emery, 78, 113, **159**

War Record of the Great Western Railway, 87, 88

War, effects on publicity (1914-18), 28, 29, 68, 86, 112, 136; (1939-45), 28, 37, 38, 76, 101, 102, 121, 129, 169; enquiries during, 156-7

Warwick, H., 29

Warwick pageant, 149

Welsh Mountain Railways, 94, 95

Westbury cut-off line, 106

White, A. J. L., 87

Wilkinson, J. L. (later Sir Joseph), 22, 25, 37

Wilkinson, Norman, 70

Williams, E. Roland, 99

Wills Ltd, 42, 84, 113

Window displays, 152

Wonderful Wessex, 84

Woodley, W. H. M., 169

Wye Valley, 124, 128